Breads You Wouldn't Believe

Easy-Do Natural Recipes Bursting With Rich Ethnic Flavor

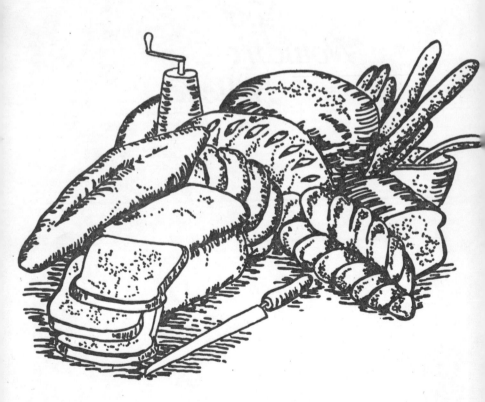

ANNE LERNER

Breads You Wouldn't Believe

CHILTON BOOK COMPANY

Radnor,
Pennsylvania

Copyright © 1974 by Royal Publications, Inc.
First Edition   *All Rights Reserved*
Published in Radnor, Pa., by Chilton Book Company
and simultaneously in Ontario, Canada
by Thomas Nelson & Sons, Ltd.

Designed by Carole L. DeCrescenzo
Manufactured in the United States of America
Second Printing, November 1974

Library of Congress Cataloging in Publication Data

Lerner, Anne.
  Breads you wouldn't believe.

  1. Bread. I. Title.
TX769.L4 1974   641.8'15   74-2466
ISBN 0-8019-5948-9
ISBN 0-8019-5952-7 (pbk.)

To NORMAN, who has opened the world of creativity to me and made this book possible.

CONTENTS

INTRODUCTION

A creative approach to bread making is an expression of moods, feelings and ideas. The results can be unbelievably interesting and rewarding. There is a challenge in the uncertainty of what is going to turn out and each attempt is really an adventure.

Many new methods of bread making have developed out of this endeavor and, indeed, several steps have brought forth a host of new bread ideas.

All these joys are within your grasp. The wonderful inner warmth created by baking your own bread and the delightful aroma that pervades the home is a welcome mat to the heart. And you'll feel a genuine satisfaction in serving health-giving nutrients to dear ones. For a child, a crusty piece of bread is a joy unequaled, manna with sweet butter and dripping honey. And many are the delights in kneading bread. It's fun working with something alive; and it's a healthy, therapeutic way to work away your tensions.

Even more, an inner cord is struck in this blessed bread making. It satisfies the soul.

A BRIEF
HISTORY OF
BREAD

The first breads were probably made from the seeds of wild grains which were ground between stones, mixed with water and spread on hot flat rocks. This process was used in the Middle East around 7000 B.C. at sites such as Jericho. Milling and baking were twin arts. The housewife crushed and ground the grain and prepared the bread or cakes. Virtually every house in Chaldea had its bread making oven in the courtyard, and the grinding stones were closeby.

The art of baking was well known in ancient Egypt. Tomb paintings portray not only planting and harvesting but grinding, bread mixing and baking as well. Actual specimens of ancient bread have been unearthed from. these burial places.

In the valley of the Nile, the Egyptians raised both barley and wheat; and for thousands of years, the flat barley cake furnished sustenance to them. Eventually, the Egyptians discovered that letting the dough of wheat ferment would make a light loaf; and this was the first real bread.

Pliny reports a crude, Roman wheat bread process. The grain was evidently powdered and the crushed remnant soaked into a pulp, made into a cake and dried in the sun. The city had no public bakers until after the war with Perseus (171-168 B.C.); it is certain that the Romans continued to make a great deal of bread at home long after public bakehouses came into use. Juvenal, in his famous satire, said that the Romans required only two things—bread and circuses. In Pompeii, several homes had private mills and bake houses. The city must also have possessed professional bakers because loaves of bread have been found, round in form and stamped with the maker's name, possibly to fix responsibility for weight and purity.

The oldest town guild of the Middle Ages was the baker's guild which had begun in the Roman Empire. Western man long ago learned to prefer raised bread to the cooked grains and flat breads; but until the last two centuries, white bread was a luxury only the wealthy could enjoy.

Over the world, bread is known by many names and is made from many grains. Scotland has its oatcake and bannoch, the latter made either from oats or barley. In Germany, the U.S.S.R. and Scandinavia, the common bread is black bread made mostly from rye, sometimes with barley or potato flour. Indians make millet cakes and chapateis from (unleavened) wheat. The Far Eastern people prefer rice to Western grains, although bread does form an increasingly large part of the diet in the Orient.

HINTS

Any one can bake bread. It's a delightful adventure and is really quite easy. Just get started and the achievement will be yours.

Every recipe has been developed individually, and I've used various methods to ensure the texture and flavor of each type of bread. Some of these procedures were devised especially so you can make your bread quickly and with few utensils.

And, of course, *it is very important to read a recipe carefully before starting.*

You can adjust ingredients such as honey and the salt to suit your taste buds.

Use the temperature closest to the one indicated in the recipe.

To Blend Mix so as to obtain a uniform product.

To Beat Stir or mix rapidly so as to make lighter. A standard kitchen tool is a slotted spoon, excellent for beating.

To Knead The usual method is to fold the dough on itself, press down with the heel of the hand, give the dough a quarter turn and repeat. Mix and work the dough into a uniform mass, usually by pressing, turning and pulling with the hands.

Yeast Fresh yeast is used in the recipes and can be purchased in a bakery. You can substitute packages of dry yeast for 1/2 oz. of fresh yeast.

Flour Do not pack down the flour when measuring. Do not sift, just spoon the flour lightly into a measuring cup. Do not shake the cup while measuring the flour.

Pans Aluminum foil pans can be obtained in hardware or supermarkets in the 3 1/4 × 5 3/4 × 2 1/4" pan size used in many of the recipes. These breads are suitable for the small family or singles.

Rising Allow the bread to rise in a warm, draft-free place. The time varies depending on the warmth of the kitchen.

Water Water should be warm to the touch when dissolving yeast.

Oil Oil your pans with a brush, using vegetable oil.

Wire Tester This is a utensil used to test if the bread is done. If the wire comes out dry, remove the bread from the oven; otherwise return to the oven for about 15 minutes more.

Abbreviations

teas.	teaspoon
tables.	tablespoon
"	inch or inches
oz.	ounce or ounces
lb.	pound.

BANANA
BREADS

Banana Batter Bread

This recipe will make a moist, attractive bread enhanced by bits of banana.

With a sharp knife, dice finely 1 1/2 bananas to measure almost 1 cup. Pour 1/2 cup of lukewarm water into a bowl. Add 1/2 oz. fresh yeast, 4 tables. vegetable oil, 2 tables. honey, 3/4 teas. salt and 1 tables. good whiskey. Stir and mix in the bananas. Beat in 1 cup of unbleached white flour. Add another 1/2 cup of flour, stirring vigorously for about 25 strokes. Gently blend in 1/2 cup of stone-ground whole wheat flour. Oil a 4 × 7 1/2 × 2″ aluminum pan. Spoon in the batter. Smooth with a spatula and set to proof in a warm place until loaf has doubled.

Turn the temperature up to 350° and bake for about 1 hour. Cool in the pan for 15 minutes. Invert on a rack. Allow to cool thoroughly before slicing.

Banana Sesame Seed Bread

Another charmer is this banana sesame seed bread, for those who want just a subtle hint of banana.

Mash 1 cup of bananas until smooth. Add the following ingredients and beat: 5 tables. vegetable oil, 1/4 cup sesame seeds, 2 tables. honey, 1 teas. salt, 1 large egg and 2 tables. wheat germ. Crumble 1/2 oz. of fresh yeast in 1/4 cup of warm water and add to the above. Mix in vigorously 1 cup of unbleached white flour. Add another cup of white flour, 1/2 cup at a time, and beat until smooth. Lastly put the dough together by working in 1/3 cup of flour. Oil a 6 1/2 × 3″ round aluminum mold. Add the dough and smooth it with oiled fingers.
Set the pan in a 200° oven (or less, if possible) or in a warm place and let rise until the dough reaches the top of the pan. Bake for about 1 hour at 350° or until golden brown. Let cool in the pan and set right side up on a wire rack.

Whole Wheat Banana Bread

Mash 2 ripe bananas well and set aside. In a bowl, put 1/2 oz. of fresh yeast in 1/2 cup of warm water and let stand for 5 minutes. Add 4 tables. vegetable oil, 1/2 teas. salt and 4 teas. of honey to the yeast mixture and stir. Blend together the bananas with the yeast mixture. Stir in rapidly 2 cups of whole wheat flour, using a slotted spoon.

Flour a board with 1/8 cup of flour. Set dough on it and spoon some of the flour on top of dough. Oil your hands and gently move the dough round and round, absorbing the flour. You may need a bit more flour (about 1 tables.), roll it till the dough is no longer sticky. Oil a 3 3/4 × 7 1/2" bread pan. Drop the dough into the pan and shake vigorously back and forth to even the dough. Oil the surface of the dough with a brush. Let rise in a warm place until 1 inch above the top of the pan.

Preheat oven to 350° and bake the bread for 50 minutes. Use a knife to ease the bread out of the pan and invert on a wire rack to cool. Cover with tinfoil and let the bread settle overnight.

BIBLICAL ~
SPIRITUAL
BREADS

Biblical Bread

And Abraham hastened into the tent unto Sarah and said: "Make ready quickly three measures of fine meal, knead it and bake cakes upon the hearth." Genesis 18:6

I can visualize Sarah making this biblical bread for a stranger at the behest of Abraham. This distinctive bread has a truly great crust which is produced by immersing a large heated stone in a pan of hot water just before the bread is set in the oven. The technique of slapping down the dough on a counter surface makes a light loaf. This bread should settle for a few hours and should be eaten fresh.

Use a medium sized bowl. Sprinkle 1/2 oz. fresh yeast in 1 1/2 cups warm water with 1 teas. of salt. Gradually add 2 1/2 cups of unbleached white flour and mix the dough lightly; it should remain somewhat lumpy. Put aside in a warm place until almost double in size, approximately 30 minutes.

Spread 1 1/2 cups of white flour on a counter; place the dough on the counter and spoon some of the flour on the top. Now pat it into the dough gently, using the tips of your fingers. Use your hands to flip the dough over several times. Add 1/4 cup of white flour and again pat it into the dough with the fingers. Fold the dough in half and use your fingers to press any remaining flour into the dough. Slap the dough down hard two times. Add 1/4 cup of white flour and repeat the above procedure. Using your palms, turn the bread round and round to shape it. Set on a 9 × 13 3/4 × 2 1/2" oiled pan. Oil the bread and allow it to become light, about 30 minutes.

Heat a large stone on the gas or electric unit for about 15 minutes. Preheat oven to 400° and set a pan of hot water in the bottom of the stove. Remove the stone from the heat with a pair of metal tongs and place in the hot water to create steam. Immediately set the bread in the oven and bake for 15 minutes. Lower the temperature to 350° and continue baking for another 40 to 50 minutes until golden and crusty. Cool on a rack.

Isaiah's Bread

And it shall come to pass in the last days, that the mountain of the Lord's house shall be firmly established on the top of the mountain.   Isaiah 2:2

And they shall beat their swords into plowshares, and their spears into pruning hooks.   Isaiah 2:4

Isaiah was a poet, a great spiritual leader, a prophet of the Hebrews who led them to redemption and brought forth God's message. He was the greatest exponent of the written word among the prophets.

This is an easy recipe. The bread has a most interesting pattern which is the result of the dough falling after it has risen, when transferred from the bread board to the baking pan.

In a bowl, make a yeast mixture by sprinkling 1/2 oz. of fresh yeast into 1/2 cup of warm water and stirring. Now add 1 teas. salt, 1 tables. vegetable oil and 2 cups of unbleached white flour. Stir with a fork to make the dough. Set the dough on a board and knead, gradually adding 1/2 cup of white flour until the flour is absorbed into the dough. It should be slightly sticky. Form into a 6" round bread on the board and let rise until nicely rounded. Transfer to an oiled 8 1/2 × 11 × 1 1/2" aluminum pan.

Preheat oven at 400° and bake for about 30 to 40 minutes. Check with a wire tester.

This bread calls for a blessing before eating it. Just break off pieces and enjoy this spiritual bread.

Joshua's Triumphant Bread

In a bowl, mix 1 cup of soy flour and 1 1/2 cups of unbleached white flour. In its center, dissolve 1/2 oz. of fresh yeast in 1/2 cup of warm water. Add 1 teas. salt, 2 tables. instant dry skim milk, 2 tables. pure peanut butter, 1/4 cup sesame seeds, 1 teas. honey, 1 teas. frozen concentrated orange juice and 1 large egg. Beat thoroughly with a slotted spoon.

Spread 3 tables. of white flour on a counter surface and knead the dough lightly, then lift and bounce it 10 times to form a ball. Oil the surface of the bread and form to fit an oiled 3 1/2 × 5 3/4 × 2 1/2" pan. Allow to proof in a warm place for about 20 minutes.

Preheat over to 350° and bake for 30 minutes. Oil the top again and bake until a golden color, about 20 minutes more. Cool on a rack.

Manna

The house of Israel named it Manna; it was like coriander seed, white, and it tasted like wafers in honey. And Moses said, "This is what the Lord has commanded. Let one omer of it be kept throughout the ages, in order that they may see the bread that I fed you in the wilderness when I brought you out from the land of Egypt."   Exodus 16: 31-32

In a perusal of the Bible, the above passage inspired me. What a meaningful word is manna! Bread making throughout the ages has been a significant part of life—the staff of life and a means of hospitality.

I wondered if I could make a manna-like bread. One Sabbath morning I discussed this with my Rabbi. He explained that manna is anything that one can imagine. I made my manna bread and it was indeed a joyful experience.

In a glass bowl, mix 1/2 oz. of fresh yeast in 1/2 cup of warm water. Add 1/2 cup of vegetable oil and 1/2 teas. of salt. Mix with a fork. Add 1 cup of unbleached white flour and stir ingredients together. Let stand for 15 minutes in a warm place. Add 1 cup of white flour, 1/4 cup at a time, alternating with 1/2 cup of warm skim milk. Use a slotted spoon to beat the ingredients together thoroughly. Oil your hands and pat the dough into an 11 × 16" aluminum cookie sheet. Pour some honey in one hand and spread on the dough. Set in a warm area for 30 minutes to proof.

Preheat oven to 350° and bake for 30 minutes or until light golden in color. Cool in the pan for 30 minutes. Cut loaf in half and, using a long knife or spatula under the bread, remove it from the pan. Cool on a rack.

CHEESE BREADS

Cheddar Cheese Bread

What fun this bread turned out to be. I was aware that my doctor hadn't been feeling well, so I decided to take him some freshly baked bread. The fun started when my busy doctor took time out to taste this bread.

Like "Old King Cole," he called for his nurse to bring him a knife. Very seriously, he cut a slice, tasted it, savored the flavor and pronounced, "It's good."

This recipe is fast and easy. It's extremely satisfying aesthetically with lovely golden curls of cheddar cheese adorning the loaf. Grate coarsely 1 cup of cheddar cheese, preferably (Longhorn type). Set aside. Let 1/2 oz. of fresh yeast dissolve in 1/2 cup of warm water for a few minutes. Meanwhile mix 1/2 teas. sugar and 1/2 teas. salt with 1 1/2 cups unbleached white flour and 1/2 cup of stone-ground whole wheat flour. Make a well and in the center pour in the yeast mixture and 1 teas. of honey. Beat and combine this together with the flour, then add the cheese. Finish mixing by squeezing the dough with your fingers.

Knead this lightly for a short time on a flat surface without adding any flour. Give it a dusting with white flour, turn it round and round with your palms. Now shape to fit an oiled 3 1/4 × 5 3/4 × 2 1/2″ pan and let rise until at least double in height.

Bake in a preheated 350° oven for 55 minutes. Bread must cool for at least 10 minutes. Invert on a rack and turn right side up.

Chive Cheese Bread

The greatest satisfaction in bread making is starting from scratch. I started this bread with a small piece of cheddar cheese. Following my thoughts, adding certain ingredients and then making changes after tasting, I finished it to satisfy my taste. This is true creativity and the way I like to work. I found after adding honey, the bread was too sweet. I then added pot cheese and chives and, in the beginning, even frozen orange juice. I was so delighted with the final result, I felt like entering it in a contest.

In a bowl dissolve 1/2 oz. of fresh yeast in 1/2 cup of warm water. Add 1 large beaten egg, 1 teas. salt, 1 teas. frozen concentrated orange juice, 1/4 cup coarsely grated cheddar cheese, 1/8 lb. melted sweet butter and 1/4 cup freeze-dried chives. Then add 1 cup unbleached white flour, 1/2 cup wheat germ and 1/2 cup whole wheat flour. Stir to make the dough.

Flatten dough on 1/4 cup of white flour on a counter. Spread surface with 1/8 cup of pot cheese, then fold the dough in half and in half again. Knead lightly to absorb the flour. Add 1/2 cup of white flour and press the flour into the dough with the fingers; turn the dough over and form into a round bread. Oil the surface and set in an oiled 9 × 13 1/4 × 2 1/2" pan. Let rise in a warm place until light, about 30 minutes.

Preheat oven to 350° and bake until delightfully golden, about 50 minutes. Check with a wire tester. Cool on a rack.

Muenster Cheese Bread

This recipe makes a very pleasing loaf and will serve a small family. For easier slicing, let it settle for several hours.

Grate 1/2 cup of muenster cheese coarsely and set aside. In a bowl, put 1/2 oz. fresh yeast, 1/2 cup warm water, 1/2 teas. salt, 1 tables. wheat germ, 1/4 cup vegetable oil, 1 tables. soy flour, 1 tables. concentrated orange juice, 1 tables. instant dry milk and 1 cup of unbleached white flour. Use an electric beater at medium speed and beat for 3 minutes. By hand, add 1 cup of white flour and blend. Set aside in a warm area for about 30 minutes until light. Add the muenster cheese.

Spoon into an oiled 3 3/4 × 7 1/2 × 2″ pan and allow to rise almost to the top of the pan. Preheat oven to 350° and set the pan without jarring. Bake for 35 to 40 minutes. Check with a wire tester. Cool.

One Bowl Dill Bread

This is a gourmet bread you will want to make; and after you've tasted it, you'll want to write home about it. It should be eaten fresh.

In a bowl, soften 1/2 oz. of fresh yeast in 1/4 cup of warm skim milk and stir. Add a pinch of raw sugar, pinch of salt and 1/2 cup of unbleached white flour. Beat the ingredients and set aside uncovered on the top of the stove or in a warm spot till it becomes spongy, about 15 minutes. Then add 1/2 cup cottage cheese, 1/4 cup sour cream, 2 teas. minced fresh dill weed, 3/4 teas. salt, 1/4 teas. raw sugar, 1 medium egg, 1 tables. wheat germ and 1 cup of flour. Blend together using a spoon. Use the edge of a knife to chop in 2 tables. of margarine. Now add 2 cups of unbleached white flour and mix, stirring lightly. Knead in the bowl with 1/2 cup of white flour, pressing this into the dough lightly with the fingers; turn the dough over and knead.

Shape into a round bread, oil the surface and set on an oiled 9 × 13 3/4 × 2 1/2" pan. Let rise in a warm place for 25 to 30 minutes. Preheat oven to 375° and bake for 45 to 55 minutes or until golden. Check with a wire tester. Cool on a rack.

Soy Cheese Bread

In a large bowl mix 1 1/4 cups unbleached white flour, 1 cup soy flour, 1 teas. salt and 2 tables. of instant dry milk. Make a depression in its center and add 1 large egg, 1/4 cup vegetable oil, 1 teas. honey, 1 teas. frozen concentrated orange juice, 2 tables. ground poppy seeds and 1/4 cup of grated provolone cheese. Next pour in 1/2 oz. of fresh yeast dissolved in 1/2 cup of warm water. With a spoon, beat the ingredients, stirring the flour from the sides of the bowl and mixing thoroughly. Pour some vegetable oil into your hands and finish mixing the dough, squeezing it with your fingers.

Knead on a board sprinkled with 3 tables. of white flour for about 5 minutes.

Form into a small oval to fit an oiled 3 1/4 × 5 3/4 × 2 1/2″ pan and allow to rise 1 inch above top of pan.

Preheat oven to 350° and bake for 40 minutes. Remove and oil the bread generously with a brush and bake for an additional 15 to 20 minutes. Cool on a rack.

Swiss Cheese Quiche Bread

Swiss cheese quiche bread is my creation, a take-off on Swiss cheese quiche pie.

In a bowl stir 1/2 cup of instant onion together with a scant 1/2 cup of coarsely grated Jolsberg Norwegian Swiss cheese. Mix in 2 well-beaten eggs, 1 teas. salt and 3 large mashed sardines. Dissolve 1/2 oz. fresh yeast in 1/2 cup warm water and 1/4 cup of beer (at room temperature) and add to the onion mixture. Blend in thoroughly and then beat 2 1/4 cups unbleached white flour, 1 teas. soy flour and 1/4 cup of wheat germ.

Spoon into an oiled 2 3/4 × 7 1/2 × 2" pan. In a warm area, let rise until the dough reaches the top of the pan. Set in a preheated 350° oven and bake for 1 hour. Check with a wire tester. Allow to cool in the pan. Remove carefully to a wire rack. Turn right side up.

CHILDREN'S
BREADS

Gregg's Gingerbread Man

"Hey, Nanna, when are we going to make a gingerbread man? I couldn't deny my five-year-old grandson this experience and that night prepared the basic ingredients. I was surprised when I mixed the water, yeast, salt and honey that the formula rose to the top of the measuring glass. I stirred in the flour, oiled the surface of the dough and set it in the refrigerator covered with wax paper.

The next morning I pushed down the yeast mixture and happily assembled some raisins and a baking pan. Gregg was out bright and early, eagerly waiting in the cold, for me to arrive. He was ready to make his gingerbread man, lickety split.

Gregg put the yeast mixture on the radiator to warm and then we located the bread board and the flour. I taught him to knead and to appreciate the smell of the yeasty dough. He put his gingerbread man together, joyfully studding him with raisins while popping half of them into his mouth. He dabbed on honey with his little fingers, licking them clean with great pleasure. After his gingerbread man was baked, he pulled off a piece and ran to watch his favorite television story.

In a bowl stir, mix and let settle for one-half hour 1/2 oz. fresh yeast, 1/4 teas. ginger, 1/3 cup warm water, 2 teas. vegetable oil, 2 teas. honey and a pinch of salt. Add 1 cup of unbleached white flour; mix together, oil surface, cover with wax paper and store in the refrigerator overnight. Push down the next morning. Allow to stand where it is warm for about 15 minutes.

On a counter surface, sprinkle 1/2 cup of white flour and knead the dough until it is smooth. Form into two gingerbread men, sprinkle the surface with brown sugar, paint a glaze with honey and stud with dark seedless raisins. Allow to rise until light, about 20 minutes.

Preheat oven at 350° and bake about 20 minutes until honey colored. Cool.

Children's Peanut Butter Bread

In a bowl sprinkle 1/2 oz. of fresh yeast in 1/2 cup of warm skim milk. Stir in thoroughly 2 tables. honey, 1/2 teas. salt and 4 tables. of natural peanut butter. Stir in 2 tables. of wheat germ and 2 1/4 cups of unbleached white flour to form the dough. Work these ingredients together with your fingers. Knead for 3 to 4 minutes on a board sprinkled with white flour and form into an oval loaf.

Place in an oiled 4 1/4 × 8 1/2 × 2″ pan and let rise until the top is 1 inch above the pan, about 30 minutes. Preheat oven to 350° and bake for 45 minutes. Cool on a rack.

Gregg's Raisin Tidbits

Gregg is my beautiful 5-year-old grandson who adores raisins and currants. He even picks them out and eats them one by one. I made this small bread for him.

I am reminded of the timeless nursery rhyme:

> Little Jack Horner
> Sat in the corner
> Eating a Christmas Pie:
> He put in his thumb,
> And pulled out a plum,
> And said, "What a good boy am I."

In a bowl dissolve 1/2 oz. of fresh yeast in 1/2 cup of warm water. Add 1/2 teas. salt, 2 tables. honey, 1/2 cup dark seedless raisins and 1 1/4 cups of unbleached white flour. Beat this for 2 minutes.

Put the dough on 1/8 cup of white flour on a counter surface. Knead for only 1 minute, pressing the flour in and gently turning the dough over and over. Turn it with your palms to form a round shape, oil the dough and set on an oiled 6 × 1″ round aluminum foil pan. Let rise in a warm place until it reaches the top of the pan, about 20 minutes.

Preheat oven to 350° and bake for 30 minutes. Cool on a rack. This is a sweet bread and the recipe can easily be doubled.

Hannah's and Lana's Gingerbread Man

I recently spent some time with two young friends in Vermont. As we dangled our feet at the edge of a shady pond, we carried on an animated conversation about a gingerbread man. What ideas poured out of these youngsters!

A baking session was planned for that very Monday. I quickly put together the initial ingredients. What fun these two young friends had making the dough, adding the necessary flour and kneading it. With much conferring, they shaped an interesting looking gingerbread man. His arms and legs were attached with much imagination and they topped him off with a final glazing of honey.

In a measuring glass dissolve 1/2 oz. of fresh yeast in 1/4 cup of warm skim milk. In a bowl mix 3/4 cup of unbleached white flour and 1 cup of whole wheat flour. Make a well and add the following ingredients: 1/4 teas. ginger, 1/2 teas. salt, 1 large beaten egg, 2 tables. brown sugar, 1 tables. honey, 1/2 teas. unsulphured molasses, 1/4 cup vegetable oil and the yeast mixture. Squeeze this with your fingers to form a round ball of dough and set this on a counter surface.

Cut off a piece of dough for the arms, legs and head. Use a larger piece for the body and attach the head, arms and legs. With your fingers, spread a glaze of honey. Stud with dark raisins for the eyes, nose and mouth. Put the gingerbread man in a 9 × 13 3/4 × 2" oiled pan and allow to rise until almost double.

Preheat oven to 350° and bake for 20 to 25 minutes until golden. Use a spatula to remove to a wire rack.

Melissa's and Reid's Chocolate Circlets

I recently went to a bakery with my grandson Reid to buy him a treat. I was amused to see his selection—a rather plain, bow shaped cookie. I made this chocolate twisted, honey-coated goodie for Reid and his sister Melissa. It's certain to charm them and satisfy their sweet tooth.

In a bowl crumble 1/2 oz. of fresh yeast in 1/2 cup of warm water. Combine 3 tables. honey, 2 tables. chocolate (I used Ghirandelli's all purpose ground chocolate), a pinch of salt, 3 tables. vegetable oil, 1 tables. wheat germ and 1 tables. of instant dry skim milk with the yeast mixture. Beat this well. Then stir in 1 cup of unbleached white flour thoroughly.

Put the dough on 1/2 cup of white flour plus 1 tables. on a counter top. Knead until the dough is flexible. Cut into 8 pieces. Roll each into a rope, twist into a circle 3 inches in diameter, pinching the ends together. Spread with oil and dip in a mixture of 1/2 teas. of cinnamon and 2 tables. of raw sugar, then paint with honey.

Set on an oiled pan, 9 × 13 3/4 × 2″, allowing space for rising. Place in a warm area for about 20 minutes until light. Preheat oven to 350° and bake until light golden in color, 30 to 35 minutes. Cool on a rack.

Patty Cake Bread

> Patty cake, patty cake,
> baker's man
> Bake me a cake
> As fast as you can;
> Roll it, pat it,
> Mark it with a B
> Put it in the oven
> For baby and me.

A child can have fun with this recipe, rolling the dough and patting it like in the rhyme.

Take 1/2 oz. of soft fresh yeast and squash it in 1/2 cup of warm milk in a bowl. Add 1 large egg, 3 tables. plus 1 teas. honey, 1/2 teas. salt and 4 teas. of sweet melted butter. Mix this in well, beating with a fork. Now add 1 3/4 cups of unbleached white flour gradually and beat for 20 strokes to form a dough. Add 1/2 cup of dark seedless raisins and press into the dough.

Let the child roll the dough back and forth on a bit of flour for a very short time, as it is sticky. Now pat into an oiled 9″ round pan and sprinkle the top with brown sugar. Set oven at 325° and bake for 30 to 40 minutes, until a delightful rich brown. Check with a wire tester. Cool on a rack.

CORN BREADS

Organic Corn Bread

There's an exhilarating rapport among people concerned with "the staff of life." Ed, a friend of mine who comes from the South, paints a nostalgic picture of his grandmother who taught him to make corn bread. Her recipe was very simple: flour, shortening, yeast and water; a homely bread with just the right human ingredient, love, to make it delicious.

In a bowl dissolve 1/2 oz. of fresh yeast in 3/4 cup of warm water. Stir in 1 teas. salt, 1 teas. unsulphured molasses, 1 1/2 cups organic corn meal, 1/2 cup whole rye flour, 4 tables. vegetable oil and 1 large egg. Beat this mixture together with a slotted spoon for 20 strokes.

On a flat surface, pour 1/2 cup of white flour and set dough there. Cover the top with some of the flour and knead gently. There should be enough flour to give the dough some body. Add about 3 tables. of white flour and knead very lightly for about 2 minutes.

Oil a 4 1/4 × 8 1/2 × 2″ pan. Oil your fingers and form the dough to fit the pan. Set in a warm area until it rises almost to the top of the pan. Bake for about 45 minutes in a 350° oven. Test with a wire tester. Cool in the pan for 10 minutes and remove to a rack.

Corn Spoon Bread

In a bowl dissolve 1/2 oz. of fresh yeast in 1 cup of warm water. Add the following ingredients and beat with an electric mixer for 2 minutes: 1 1/2 cups organic corn meal, 1 cup unbleached white flour, 1 large egg, 1/2 teas. salt, 1/4 lb. melted margarine and 2 tables. of honey.

Pour mixture in an oiled loaf pan 3 3/4 × 7 1/2 × 2". Put in a warm place and allow to increase in volume to just below the top of the pan.

Bake in a preheated 350° oven for 30 minutes. Lower temperature to 250° and continue baking until light golden. Cool slightly. Serve from the pan with a spoon. This is a delicate, light bread.

Quick, Intriguing
Corn Bread

This is indeed a quick and intriguing bread. It is very light and should be eaten fresh.

In a bowl dissolve 1/2 oz. of fresh yeast in 1/2 cup of warm skim milk. Add 2 tables. honey, 1 teas. frozen concentrated orange juice, 1/2 teas. salt, 4 tables. vegetable oil, 1/2 cup whole wheat flour and 1/2 cup of organic corn meal. Beat with a slotted spoon for 20 strokes. Lastly, with a spoon, beat in 1 large egg and 1 cup of unbleached white flour for 1 minute.

Spoon mixture into a generously oiled 3 3/4 × 7 1/2 × 2" pan. Allow to rise to the top of the pan. Preheat oven to 350° and bake for 40 to 50 minutes until a rich golden color. Cool in pan and remove carefully.

DESSERT
BREADS

Blueberry Bread

Blueberries are a perennial favorite, but unfortunately the season is very short. Some time ago, I developed a blueberry bread thinking that it would be my only one. One afternoon, Peg and Ed Fitzgerald, who broadcast on the radio, were discussing a blueberry bread that a friend had sent Ed. It was sampled by two other members of his household and he was explaining how really good it was. I just had to make another blueberry bread. This bread can be made quickly and freezes exceptionally well.

In a bowl measure 1/4 cup of warm skim milk and stir in 1/2 oz. of fresh yeast. Add 2 tables. melted margarine, 1/2 teas. salt, 1 large egg, 1 tables. wheat germ, 2 tables. honey and 2 cups of unbleached white flour. Stir this thoroughly. Fold in 1 cup of blueberries. In a warm place, let rise for 20 minutes.

Spoon mixture on a floured patch (about 1/4 cup) on a counter surface and stir with a knife to mix the dough. Then using the hands, roll it back and forth several times. Oil the dough and set in a 3 1/2 × 5 3/4 × 2 1/2" pan and let rise until almost double.

Preheat oven to 375° and bake for about 40 minutes. Check with a wire tester. Cool on a rack.

Goldencurl
Coconut Bread

Marco Polo was one of the first Europeans to describe coconuts. They're very common in the Caribbean islands. A high protein food, the locals use them in many ways. After learning this, I hurried to my local supermarket and bought one. That day after work, I made a coconut bread that I have been told is delectable.

Punch three holes in the coconut with a sharp instrument and pour the coconut milk into a measuring cup. Use 1/2 cup of the milk for this recipe. Put the coconut in a heavy bag and bang very hard on a solid surface to break the shell. Dissolve 1/2 oz. of fresh yeast in 1/4 cup of warm skim milk. Add 1 cup coarsely grated coconut, grated rind of an orange, 3 tables. vegetable oil, 1/8 cup raw sugar, 3/4 teas. salt, 1 large beaten egg and the coconut milk. With a spoon, beat in 1 1/8 cups of unbleached white flour until thoroughly mixed.

Spread 1 cup plus 2 tables. of white flour on a board and roll the dough back and forth lightly. Now press the dough with the tips of the fingers so it absorbs the flour. Bounce several times. Sprinkle with white flour. Turn round and round with your palms.

Oil the dough with a brush and set on an oiled baking pan 9 × 13 3/4 × 2 1/2". Let rise for about 30 minutes until light. Mix 1/2 cup grated coconut with 2 tables. brown sugar and 2 tables. of vegetable oil. Sprinkle this on top.

Preheat oven to 350° and bake for 40 to 50 minutes. Check with a wire tester. Cool on a rack.

Poppy Seed Bread/Cake

The dried seed of the poppy plant was known to the Egyptians before 1500 B.C. One species of the poppy was developed by the Dutch for its delightful aromatic seed. In their province of Zeeland, the great skill of cultivating this plant for its walnut-flavored, delectable seed is handed down, with great pride, from one family generation to the next.

In a warm bowl measure 1/2 cup of warm water and stir in 1/2 oz. of fresh yeast until dissolved. Combine 3 tables. honey, 4 tables. raw sugar, 2 tables. melted margarine, 1 large egg, 3/4 cup currants, 1 tables. wheat germ and 1 teas. of salt. Add 1 cup of unbleached white flour and stir rapidly with a slotted spoon. Blend in another cup of white flour with 1 cup of poppy seeds to form the dough.

Spread 1/4 cup of white flour on a board and knead the dough until it is somewhat sticky. Add 1/8 cup of white flour and knead for a short time, turning the dough round and round.

Form into a round shape, set in an oiled 3 3/4 × 7 1/2 × 2″ pan and let rise.

Preheat oven to 375° and bake for 40 to 50 minutes. Test with a wire tester. Cool on a rack.

Sunshine Bread

In a bowl dissolve 1/2 oz. fresh yeast in 1/4 cup warm water with 1/4 cup of warm orange juice. Add 1 large egg, 2 teas. vanilla flavor, grated rind of an orange, 1/2 teas. salt, 4 tables. vegetable oil, 2 tables. honey, 1 tables. wheat germ and 4 tables. of cranberry sauce. Use a slotted spoon to beat in 2 cups of unbleached white flour, 1 cup at a time for 25 strokes. Add 1/4 cup of white flour and stir to blend.

Flour a counter with 1/4 cup of white flour and set the dough there. Flatten it and press the flour into it. Knead for a short time, adding, if necessary, enough flour to handle the dough well. Bounce it to make a cohesive ball and shape with the hands. Let rest for 10 minutes on the board and then remove carefully to an oiled 9 × 13 3/4 × 2 1/2″ pan.

Set the pan in a 250° oven, turn on the heat and bake for 15 minutes. Increase temperature to 350° and bake for 15 minutes more. Increase temperature to 375° and bake for 15 minutes. Finish baking bread at 400° until it is well baked, about 10 minutes more. Check with a wire tester. Cool on a rack. This bread should split in the center.

Al's Cinnamon
Raisin Bread

A welcome telephone call from my brother Al, who had just returned from the South, was my inspiration for this recipe. After the usual preliminary greetings, he asked me what I was doing. I told him I was busy with my bread cookbook.

He went on, "I want to tell you about a bread that I liked very much in Florida, a raisin cinnamon bread that was really good. And it didn't have too much cinnamon in it. For my breakfast every morning, I toasted it and spread it with cream cheese."

As he was talking, my mind was busy thinking, and I told him that I was going to make such a bread.

Measure 1/2 cup of warm water in a bowl and stir in 1/2 oz. of fresh yeast. The following ingredients are added and beaten together with the yeast mixture: 1 teas. salt, 2 tables. honey, 4 tables. vegetable oil, 1 teas. cinnamon, 2 tables. wheat germ and 1 cup of unbleached white flour. Mix in 1 cup of dark seedless raisins. Blend in 1 cup of white flour.

On a counter, spread 1/2 cup of white flour, and knead the dough for about 5 minutes. Form into a round loaf, oil the surface and set into an oiled 3 3/4 × 7 1/2 × 2″ pan and let double in a warm place.

Preheat oven to 375° and bake for about 45 minutes. Check with a wire tester.

Horseshoe Coffee Ring

Why go out to a bakery for a coffee ring? You can make one quickly for unexpected guests or the family, using leftover coffee for flavoring.

In a bowl crumble 1/2 oz. of fresh yeast in 1/2 cup of warm skim milk. Add 6 tables. warm coffee, 6 teas. raw sugar, 2 tables. honey, 2 oz. soft margarine, grated rind of an orange, 1/2 teas. salt and 1 large beaten egg. Add 2 cups of unbleached white flour, 1 cup at a time, and beat for 20 strokes. Blend in 1/2 cup of currants.

Spread 1/2 cup plus 3 tables. of wheat germ on a counter surface and scoop the dough onto the counter. Now use a spoon to blend this together. Lift and bounce the dough a few times. You will find it semi-soft. The next step is to add 1/4 cup of white flour and knead it into a soft dough.

Oil a 9 × 13 3/4 × 2 1/2″ pan. Oil the dough and set on the pan. Shape into a 5″ wide horseshoe. Brush the surface with honey. Allow to proof in a warm place until light, about 20 minutes or until the dough spreads.

Preheat oven to 350° and bake for 40 minutes until golden. Allow to cool in the pan before removing to a rack.

Apple Bread

This apple bread is a light textured, delicious bread which is certain to be popular with the family for dessert.

To hasten the rising of the bread, pour hot water in a mixing bowl and let stand for a few minutes. Pour out the water. Heat 1/2 cup of skim milk just below the boiling point. Add 4 tables. of margarine. Allow to cool for 5 minutes and pour into the bowl. Stir in 1/2 oz. fresh yeast, 5 teas. raw sugar and 1/2 teas. of salt. Beat in 1 cup of unbleached white flour with a slotted spoon for several minutes. Combine 1 cup diced apples, 1 tables. pineapple juice, 3 tables. raw sugar and 1 cup unbleached white flour to the yeast mixture and stir together.

Spoon this into an oiled 3 3/4 × 7 1/2 × 2″ loaf pan. Oil the top of the dough and allow to rise to the top of the pan.

Preheat oven to 375° and bake for 40 minutes. Test with a wire. Cool in the pan.

Cinnamon Orange Coffee Cake/Bread

In a bowl dissolve 1/2 oz. fresh yeast in 1/2 cup warm water with 1 teas. salt. Stir and beat 4 tables. brown sugar, 2 large eggs, 2 teas. cinnamon, grated rind of an orange and 1/3 cup of vegetable oil. Using a slotted spoon, mix in 2 cups of unbleached white flour then beat vigorously for several strokes.

Sprinkle 1 cup of white flour on a board. Set the dough there and knead, pressing the fingers into the dough, gathering the flour and then kneading with the heel of the hands until the flour is absorbed. Bounce the dough several times. Shape into an oval and oil the surface. Set in an oiled 2 × 8 1/2 × 4 1/4" pan and allow to double.

Preheat oven to 350° and bake for about 45 minutes. Check with a wire tester. Remove to a rack to cool.

Cinnamon Tea Loaf

In bowl of electric mixer, combine 1/2 oz. fresh yeast, 1/2 cup warm water, 4 tables. margarine, 1 large egg, 1/2 teas. salt, 3 tables. brown sugar and 1 teas. of cinnamon. Beat at medium speed for 1 minute. Add 1 cup of unbleached white flour and then beat at a slow speed for 1 minute. Add another cup of white flour and 1/2 cup of seedless raisins. Now use a wooden spoon to mix the dough.

Turn out the dough on 1/2 cup plus 1 tables. of white flour and knead, pressing with the fingers until the flour is absorbed. Let rest for 10 minutes. Bounce the dough a few times.

Oil a 3 3/4 × 7 1/2 × 2 1/2″ pan and set the dough in gently. Allow to rise to the top of the pan.

Preheat oven to 350° and bake for 35 to 45 minutes. Check with a wire tester. Cool on a wire rack.

Yogurt Orange
Coffee Cake/Bread

In a bowl dissolve 1/2 oz. fresh yeast in 1/4 cup fresh orange juice with 1/4 teas. salt and 1/4 teas. of raw sugar. Beat in 1/2 cup of unbleached white flour. Set in a warm place for 10 minutes. Add 4 tables. melted butter, 1 tables. wheat germ, 1/4 cup yogurt, 4 1/2 tables. honey, 1/2 teas. salt and 1 large beaten egg. Beat vigorously with a fork. Add 1 1/2 cups of unbleached white flour and stir.

Set dough on a patch with 1/2 cup of white flour on a counter surface. Press dough into the flour with the fingers, turning it over and repeating until all the flour is absorbed.

Shape into a round loaf, oil the surface and place in an oiled 3 3/4 ×5 3/4 × 2 1/4" pan. Let rise until double. Preheat oven to 400° and bake for 30 minutes until golden. Cool in the pan. Turn out on a wire rack.

Sunrise Apple Bread

In a bowl measure 1/4 cup warm water and stir in 1/4 oz. fresh yeast, 1/2 teas. raw sugar and 1/2 teas. of salt. Add 1/2 cup coarsely grated apples, 1 tables. wheat germ, 3 tables. brown sugar and 1/4 teas. of mace. Cut in 2 tables. of margarine. Now add 1 1/2 cups of unbleached white flour and stir thoroughly.

Set the dough on a patch of 1/2 cup of white flour. Knead lightly for about 2 minutes and form to fit an oiled 3 1/4 × 5 3/4 × 2 1/2" pan. Let rise until light in a warm place, for about 20 minutes.

Preheat oven to 375° and bake for 30 to 35 minutes. Check with a wire tester. Cool on a rack.

Nut Bread

In a bowl make a well in 2 1/4 cups of unbleached white flour. In the center put 1/2 oz. of fresh yeast and stir this with 1/2 cup of warm water. Add 3 egg yolks, 1 tables. frozen concentrated orange juice, 1/2 teas. salt, grated rind of a small lemon, 3 tables. honey, 2 tables. brown sugar and 2 tables. of wheat germ. Beat the center ingredients with a fork then mix in the flour until thoroughly blended. Stir in 1/2 cup of ground walnuts.

Oil a 3 3/4 × 7 1/2 × 2" pan and spoon the dough in. Set in a warm area and let the dough rise until 1 inch above the top of the pan. Preheat oven to 350° and bake for 45 to 55 minutes. Check with a wire tester. Cool on a rack.

Whole Wheat Popovers

In a large bowl, dissolve 1/2 oz. fresh yeast in 1/2 cup warm water with 1 teas. of salt. Beat in 1/4 cup vegetable oil, 2 tables. honey and 2 large beaten eggs. Beat in 2 cups of unbleached white flour. Blend in 1 cup of organic whole wheat flour.

Spread oil in 8 muffin tins and spoon the dough three-quarters full. Let rise for 10 to 20 minutes in a warm place. With a fork, peak the tops and let double in volume.

Preheat oven to 425° and bake for about 15 minutes until a golden color. Cool in the pan.

Blueberry Kuchen

Make a well in 2 1/4 cups of unbleached white flour in a bowl. Crumble in 1/2 oz. of fresh yeast in 1/2 cup of warm water and stir. Add 4 teas. raw sugar, 1/2 teas. salt, 1 large egg and 2 tables. of margarine. Using a knife, pound the margarine in with the ingredients and stir to form the dough. Set aside in a warm place for 30 minutes. Put the dough into an oiled 2 × 8 1/4″ square pyrex baking dish and pat to fit evenly.

Mix 2 cups fresh blueberries with 1 teas. lemon juice and 2 tables. of raw sugar and spread evenly on the dough. Fold the long side of the dough to the center, one end overlapping the other. Tuck the ends under. Oil the surface with your fingers. Allow to rise in a warm place for about 20 to 25 minutes.

Preheat oven to 360° and bake 30 to 40 minutes until light brown. Cool in the dish.

One Bowl Cinnamon Raisin Bread

The ancient Hebrews and Egyptians used the oils of cinnamon in rituals and sacred ceremonies. It is one of the oldest spices and its history can be traced back to 5000 B.C.

Everything can be mixed in one bowl to save time.
Dissolve 1/2 oz. of fresh yeast in 1/2 cup of warm water. Add 1 teas. of salt and 4 tables. of brown sugar. Stir in 2 cups unbleached white flour, 2 large eggs, 1/3 cup vegetable oil and 2 teas. of cinnamon. Beat with a spoon, gathering the flour into the mixture. Add 1 1/4 cups of white flour, the rind of an orange and 3/4 cup of dark raisins. Use your fingers to mix the dough.
Shape into an oval loaf. Oil the dough and set in an oiled foil pan 2 × 8 1/2 × 4 1/4″ and let rise in a warm place until the bread reaches the top of the pan.
Preheat oven to 350° and bake for 30 to 40 minutes. Cool on a rack.

Raisin Tea Loaf

A loquacious Irish lady told me about a special Irish cake made with raisins soaked in tea. This loaf has a light texture and will rise quite high.

In a bowl soak 1/2 cup of seedless dark raisins in 1/2 cup of strong hot tea. When the mixture cools, crumble in 1/2 oz. of fresh yeast and mix. Then add 1/2 teas. salt, 1/3 cup raw sugar, 1 large egg and 1 teas. of vanilla flavoring. Stir in 1 cup of unbleached white flour with a fork until well blended. Then combine 1/4 cup of melted sweet butter and the last cup of white flour thoroughly.

Spoon dough into an oiled 3 3/4 × 7 1/2 × 2" pan and allow to rise to the top of the pan in a warm area. Preheat oven to 375° and bake for about 35 minutes. Check with a wire tester. Allow to cool in the pan and then remove to a wire rack.

Whole Wheat
Raisin Muffins

In a bowl crumble 1/2 oz. fresh yeast, add 3/4 cup warm water, 1/4 cup vegetable oil, 1/2 teas. salt and 1 teas. of brown sugar and mix. Add 1 3/4 cups of stone-ground whole wheat flour and beat thoroughly. Stir in 3/4 cup of seedless raisins and blend.

Oil 8 large muffin cups and fill equally. Allow to rise to the top of the pan, approximately 15 to 20 minutes. Preheat oven to 400° and bake for 20 to 30 minutes until medium golden. Cool in the pan and turn out on a rack.

FRENCH BREADS

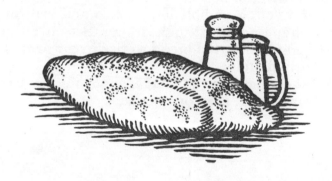

Fun French Bread

I cannot overemphasize the therapeutic value of bread making for relieving tension. There is utter enjoyment in mixing and manipulating the dough, lifting and bouncing and finally achieving the right texture.

In a bowl stir 3 cups unbleached white flour together with 1 1/2 teas. salt and 3 tables. of wheat germ and make a depression. In its center mix 1/2 oz. of fresh yeast with 1 cup of warm water. Using a slotted spoon, slowly work the flour in from the sides of the bowl and then beat the mixture vigorously, until thoroughly stirred together. This is a sticky dough.

Flour a board with 3/4 cup of white flour plus 2 tables. and turn out the dough. Use a spoon to turn it over and over to coat it, then knead thoroughly, pressing down with the heel of the hands.

Fold the dough in half lengthwise and roll into a narrow shape about 12 inches long. Set on an oiled 11 × 16″ pan. Allow the bread to rise in a warm place until nearly double.

Preheat oven to 375° and bake for 45 minutes. Check with a wire tester. Cool on a rack.

Gloria's French Bread

Use a bowl and dissolve 1/2 oz. of fresh yeast in 3/4 cup of warm water. Add 1 teas. of salt and stir. Mix in 2 cups of unbleached white flour stirring vigorously with a slotted spoon.

Spread 1 1/4 cups of white flour on a counter surface. Set the dough on it. Use the side of a spoon to mix the dough with the flour and knead gently for about 2 minutes. Shape into a round bread and set on an oiled 9 × 13 3/4 × 2 1/2" pan. Allow to proof in a warm area for about 20 minutes.

Preheat oven to 375° and bake for 30 minutes. Check with a wire tester. Cool on a rack.

Happy Crusty
French Bread

Have you ever watched Julia Child's program? I was invited to watch it at the home of a friend. I was completely absorbed and interested in Julia's bread but aware that it was very complicated. No bread was going to throw me. Why be bothered with a complicated procedure? You must approach this endeavor with a relaxed and happy attitude, and even the bread will grow with contentment. Just try it and see. Smell the bread while it is rising; you'll love the yeasty aroma.

Use a medium-size glass bowl rinsed in hot water. Dissolve 1/2 oz. of fresh yeast in 1/2 cup of warm water. Add 1 teas. salt, 2 tables. vegetable oil and 1/4 teas. of raw sugar. Stir together. With a slotted spoon, beat in 1 3/4 cups of unbleached white flour. Combine 1/2 cup of white flour with the other ingredients and stir together. Set aside for 15 to 20 minutes in a warm area.

Flour a board with about 3/4 cup of white flour and knead until the dough is no longer sticky. Flatten it, using your palms; then fold in half and in half again. Roll until it is 10 1/2 inches long. Sprinkle corn meal on a 11 × 16" cookie sheet and set the dough. Use a brush to oil the surface. Slash the top about 1/2 inch deep across the loaf with a sharp knife and allow to proof, about 30 minutes.

Preheat oven to 375° and bake for 20 minutes. Remove from oven and spread the surface with water, using a brush. Continue to bake for 30 to 35 minutes. Cool on a rack.

FRIENDSHIP
BREADS

Claire's Bread

I gave this bread to a friend who is a gourmet. She thought it was the best bread I had ever made.

In a bowl dissolve 1/2 oz. of fresh yeast in 1/2 cup of light warm peach syrup. Stir in 1 teas. brandy flavoring, 2 teas. honey, 6 tables. instant dry skim milk, 4 tables. vegetable oil, 1/2 teas. salt and 1/4 cup of chopped walnuts. Stir in rapidly 1 1/2 cups of unbleached white flour to make a dough.

Set the dough on a counter surface in the center of 3/4 cup of white flour. Knead for a few minutes, then use your fingers to further mix the dough by squeezing it. Bounce the dough several times. Form into a small round bread and set in a 9" oiled round pan. Oil the surface. Let double in a warm place.

Preheat oven to 350° and bake for about 1 hour. Test with a wire tester. Cool on a rack.

Meta's Ground
Poppy Seed Loaf

In a bowl dissolve 1/2 oz. fresh yeast in 1 cup warm
water with 1 teas. of salt. Beat in 2 tables. honey, 8
tables. vegetable oil, 2 large eggs and 1 teas. of fresh
lemon juice. Stir in 3 cups of unbleached white flour
and 1/2 cup of ground poppy seeds with the yeast
mixture; then stir vigorously with a slotted spoon for
20 strokes.

Make a patch of 1 cup of white flour on a counter
surface and set dough there. Knead for 5 minutes.
Shape the dough into an oval loaf and oil the surface.

Set in a generously oiled bread pan 5 1/2 × 9 1/2 ×
2 3/4". Let it double in bulk. Preheat oven to 350° and
bake for about 1 hour. Check with a wire tester and cool
across the top of the pan.

Norman's Moon Glow
Health Bread

This was my lovely surprise last night: a bread that didn't require any preliminary rising. I made this bread for a special friend who has influenced me in my creativity. This appetizing bread can be used as a centerpiece at a dinner party and served with fruit and cheese.

Heat 1/2 cup of orange juice until lukewarm and then pour into a deep bowl. Stir in 1/2 oz. of fresh yeast, 1 heaping tables. wheat germ, 1 heaping tables. instant dry skim milk, 1 tables. soy flour, 1 large egg, 1 teas. olive oil, 3 tables. vegetable oil, 1 tables. unsulphured blackstrap molasses, 1 teas. salt, 1/4 teas. sugar and 1/8 cup of canned, sweetened pineapple juice. Beat all this very well with a fork. Combine with 1 1/4 cups of unbleached white flour and set aside in a warm place until the mixture bubbles. Stir in 1/4 cup of whole wheat flour.

Make a patch of 1 cup of whole wheat flour on a counter surface. Set the dough there and knead until sticky. Then stretch the dough with oiled fingers, pulling it like taffy for several minutes and finish kneading with about 1/8 cup of white flour, until the dough is semi-firm. It will be slightly sticky.

Oil the dough, shape into three round balls and set them close together on an oiled 9 × 13 3/4 × 2 1/2″ pan. Preheat oven to 350° and bake bread for about 1 hour. Check with a wire tester. Cool on a rack.

Pearl's Wonder Bread

In a bowl stir 1/2 oz. of fresh yeast in 1/2 cup of warm water. Beat in 1 teas. salt, 1 teas. brown sugar, 1 cup unbleached white flour and 2 tables. of honey. Set aside to rise in a warm place for 15 minutes. Put in 2 large beaten eggs, 1/2 cup vegetable oil, 2 tables. instant dry skim milk and 1 cup of whole wheat flour and stir.

On a counter surface, make a patch of 1 1/8 cups of white flour and set dough there. Use a spoon to mix this since it is soft, and afterwards use your hands to press and roll the dough over and over to gather all the flour into the dough. Oil the surface. Shape gently into a round loaf. Set on an oiled 9 × 13 3/4 × 2 1/2" pan and let double in size.

Preheat oven to 350° and bake for 35 to 45 minutes. Check with a wire tester. Cool on a rack.

Rey's Orange Bread

Returning from Vermont along the scenic Taconic Parkway, we passed the time viewing the scenery, eating, dozing and sharing ideas. People always have something to say about what they like to eat. My friend Rey likes orange peel and Meta, his wife, likes ground poppy seeds in any form. No sooner did I arrive home, I hastened to the refrigerator for the Jaffa orange marmalade from Israel to make Rey's bread. This bread is excellent served with cream cheese.

In a bowl dissolve 1/2 oz. of fresh yeast in 1/2 cup of warm orange juice. Beat in 2 cups unbleached white flour, 1 large egg, 1 teas. salt, 2 tables. instant dry skim milk, grated rind of an orange, 2 tables. vegetable oil and 4 tables. of orange marmalade.

Spoon this dough into an oiled 3 3/4 × 7 1/2 × 2″ pan. Oil the top and let rise until the dough reaches the top of the pan. Preheat oven to 375° and bake for 30 to 40 minutes until a light golden color. Check with a wire tester. Cool in the pan for 10 minutes. Remove to a rack. Allow the bread to settle before slicing.

FUN AND
JOYOUS
BREADS

Aphrodisiac Bread

Who ever heard of an aphrodisiac bread? This is how it came about. My son-in-law Stanley told me about a television program he had recently seen featuring an authoress who spoke about her aphrodisiac cookbook. "Why don't you make an aphrodisiac bread, Anne?" That started it. My daughter thought it a good idea, and so did a friend who said, "Believe me Anne, this is just what I need."

An aphrodisiac bread is for those who want to have a memorable evening at home. You'll have an extra treat awaiting you the next time you invite someone to "Come with me to the Casbah."

This exotic bread has curry powder, garlic and herbs and is quite light in texture.

In a large bowl sprinkle 1/2 oz. of fresh yeast in 1/2 cup of warm water and dissolve. Add 1 1/2 cups unbleached white flour, 2 tables. vegetable oil, 1/2 teas. curry powder, 2 pinches of parsley flakes, 3/4 teas. salt and 1 teas. of minced garlic and beat well with a fork.

Spread 1/2 cup plus 1 tables. of white flour on a counter surface and set dough there. Knead lightly for 5 minutes. Form into a round bread. Oil the surface. Let rise until double in a 8 1/2 × 11 × 1 1/2" pan.

Preheat oven to 350° and bake for 45 minutes until light brown. Cool on a rack.

Aromatic Bread

Anise dates as far back as 1500 B.C. It was listed among the medicinal herbs of the Egyptians. Centuries later Pliny wrote glowingly of the flavor of anise leaves and seeds. Anise found its way to England like so many of the ancient herbs used by the Romans. During medieval times, it was one of the highly taxed, imported herbs. The first American colonists brought anise from England, and it has remained a favorite ever since.

Stanley's suggestion of an aromatic flavor for my aphrodisiac bread brought about my aromatic bread with anise flavoring.

In a warm bowl, press 1/2 oz. of fresh yeast in 1/2 cup of warm water and dissolve. Make a depression in a mixture of 1 cup of unbleached white flour and 1 cup of whole wheat flour. In its center put the yeast mixture, 1 1/2 teas. anise flavor, 1 teas. vanilla flavor, 1 teas. salt, 1/4 cup vegetable oil and 1 large egg. Beat together with a slotted spoon.

Make a patch of 3/4 cup of white flour on a counter surface and set dough there. Knead for a short time; the dough should not be sticky. Shape into a round form and allow to rise until double in an oiled pan 8 1/2 × 11 × 1 1/2".

Preheat oven to 375° and bake for 30 to 40 minutes until it is the color of honey. Check with a wire tester. Cool.

Carrot Bread

There were three rather limp carrots in the bottom of my refrigerator—what to do with them? A carrot bread of course. The oven temperature for this little bread was a serious matter—an affair of state almost. It was settled by degrees.

In a bowl mix 1/2 oz. of fresh yeast in 1/2 cup of warm orange juice. Add 2 tables. honey, 1 teas. salt, 2 tables. vegetable oil and 1 cup of unbleached white flour. Stir. Then mix in 1 cup of coarsely grated carrots and 2 large beaten eggs. Blend in 2 1/8 cups of wheat germ. Form into an oval.

Place in an oiled 4 1/4 × 8 1/2 × 2" aluminum foil pan. Let rise to the top of the pan. Set in the oven at 200° and bake for 20 minutes. Increase temperature to 250° and continue baking for 15 minutes, raise temperature to 350° and finish baking for 25 minutes. Check with a wire tester. Cool on a rack.

Citron Bread
Panettone

Frank is a dear friend of mine. He is now retired and spends his time painting. Rarely do I visit him without bringing one of my breads. Frank comes from a small town in the southern part of Italy where it is the custom to serve *panettone* at Christmas for breakfast. "Why don't you buy *panettone?*" he suggested after this reminiscence. This convulsed me—it was like bringing coals to New Castle. "Oh I know, you want to make your own bread. Go to the Italian section around Thanksgiving and buy citron when it is fresh," he added.

I suggest that only fresh citron be used.

In a bowl dissolve 1/2 oz. of fresh yeast in 1/4 cup of warm water. Then add 2 egg yolks, 1 tables. gin, 1 cup dark seedless raisins, 2 tables. soft margarine, 1 teas. salt, 1 teas. almond flavoring, 1 teas. brandy flavoring and 3/4 cups of diced citron. Add 1 1/2 cups of un-bleached white flour and stir.

Put 1/2 cup plus 3 tables. of white flour on a counter, set the dough there and turn it over and over into the flour. Knead it gently, pressing down lightly for 1 or 2 minutes until the dough becomes sticky. Sprinkle the dough with flour. Oil your hands and turn it to make a round form for an oiled 9″ pie pan. Allow to become light, about 20 minutes.

Preheat oven to 350° and bake for 40 to 45 minutes. Check with a wire tester. Cool on a rack.

Five-Minute
Onion Bread

The onion originated in Asia and this pungent herb has been one of my favorites. Homer considered it a rare delicacy.

The idea for this onion bread germinated in my mind for a whole month. It was my young friend Lana who shyly suggested this bread when we were together in Vermont. I asked her, "What would you put into it?" There was a long pause; I prodded her a little. "Would you like some sliced onions in it?" "Mmmm, yes—it would be good that way."

In a bowl mix 1/2 cup of freshly grated onion with 1 teas. of salt. Add 1/2 oz. of fresh yeast dissolved in 1/2 cup of warm water. Then add 2 1/2 cups of unbleached white flour and 1/4 cup of vegetable oil and beat well.

Spoon the dough into an oiled 3 3/4 × 7 1/2 × 2" baking pan. Let the dough rise to the top of the pan. Preheat oven to 350° and bake for 1 hour. Check with a wire tester. Invert on a rack to cool. Turn the bread right side up.

Gladsome Oatmeal Bread

This is super nutritious bread which gladdened my thrifty heart, using up the last of my oatmeal.

In a bowl dissolve 1/2 oz. of fresh yeast in 1 cup of warm water. Now add 1 teas. salt, 2 tables. honey, 2 tables. unsulphured molasses, 2 tables. instant dry skim milk, 3 large beaten eggs, 1/3 cup vegetable oil and 2 cups of whole grain rolled oats. Mix thoroughly with a slotted spoon and set aside for 30 minutes in a warm place. Add gradually 2 cups of whole wheat flour, mixing and stirring the ingredients until the dough holds together. Lift and bounce on the counter several times.

Form into a round bread and set on an oiled 5 1/2 × 9 1/2 × 2 3/4" bread pan. Allow to double in a warm place for 30 minutes. Preheat oven to 350° and bake for 50 minutes until light golden. Cool in the pan for 10 minutes. Remove to a rack to cool.

Master Chef Bread

I was so excited by this bread, I felt like parading it around. It grew so beautifully—I want to find the right words to describe this grateful feeling. Come everybody, look at this gorgeous Challa. I wanted to call in my neighbors, to share this experience.

In a large bowl grate the rind of a small lemon. Dissolve 1/2 cup of warm water with 1/2 oz. of fresh yeast. Add to the lemon rind 1 teas. lemon juice, 1/2 cup vegetable oil, 1 teas. salt, 3 tables. honey and 2 large eggs. Beat this well with a fork. Add 2 cups of unbleached white flour and with a slotted spoon mix vigorously about 20 strokes. Mix an additional 1 1/2 cups of white flour with the side of the spoon. Now use your fingers to pull the dough like taffy for 5 minutes.

Make a patch of 1/2 cup plus 1 tables. of white flour on a flat surface. Set the dough on it and knead for about 5 minutes until the dough is smooth. Now cut the dough into three equal parts. Roll each piece into a strand 8 inches long and braid. Set on an oiled 9 × 13 3/4 × 2 1/2″ pan and spread the surface with part of a well beaten egg. Sprinkle with poppy seeds.

Let rise in a warm place until double in bulk. Bake in a preheated 400° oven for 20 minutes. Lower temperature to 350° and bake for 25 minutes more. Cool on a rack.

Molasses Bread

Despite an editor's deadline, a friend who is writing an English textbook came to visit from New York City. When she heard I was writing a cookbook, she made this comment to my surprise, "A cookbook is better than sex." "What do you mean Elsie?" Roaring with laughter she gasped, "I meant cookbooks sell better than sex books." Elsie is an advocate of health foods and is enthusiastic about a bread she buys which will stay fresh for 2 weeks in the refrigerator.

Unsulphured molasses has many nutrients such as thiamin, riboflavin and niacin. The molasses bread has a soft texture and stays fresh in the refrigerator for 2 weeks, if it lasts that long.

In a bowl dissolve 1/2 oz. of fresh yeast in 1/2 cup of warm orange juice. Mix and add 2 large eggs, 2 tables. honey, 4 tables. vegetable oil, 2 tables. unsulphured blackstrap molasses, 1 teas. salt, 1/2 cup soy flour, 1/2 cup organic corn meal and 1 1/2 cups of whole wheat flour. Beat this batter with a slotted spoon for about 25 strokes.

Oil a loaf pan 3 3/4 × 7 1/2 × 2" and spoon in the dough. Let rise to the top of the pan. Preheat oven to 350° and bake for about 45 minutes. Test with a wire tester. Cool in the pan. Invert on a rack.

Pistol Packing Mama Bread

This bread was made for a special mama, Golda Meir, Prime Minister of Israel. What a spirit she has! The bread was the result of an article in the *New York Times* about her and Indira Gandi as "pistol packing mamas" of their countries. I wrote to Golda Meir and told her about my "Pistol Packing Mama Bread" and my desire to help Israel. A reply from her office is one of my proud possessions.

This lovely persimmon-colored bread has a garlicky spirit and the essence of many flavors. It is a pizza-like bread and is quite tasty when served warm.

Warm 1/2 cup of seasoned tomato sauce. Stir in 1/2 oz. fresh yeast, 2 teas. garlic powder, 3/4 teas. salt, a generous pinch of parsley flakes, 1/4 teas. basil, 8 tables. Parmesan cheese and 3 tables. of vegetable oil. Beat this mixture well with a spoon and set aside in a warm place for about 15 to 20 minutes.

In a bowl stir 2 1/4 cups of unbleached white flour with the yeast mixture. Add 1/4 cup of warm water and beat vigorously with a slotted spoon for 25 strokes, for a light dough. Put 1/2 cup of white flour on a counter surface and set the dough on it. Knead for about 5 minutes.

Oil the surface and turn the dough to form a round shape. Let double in size in an oiled 9 × 13 3/4 × 2 1/2″ pan. Preheat oven to 375° and bake for 30 to 45 minutes. Check with a wire tester. Cool on a rack.

Potpourri Bread

While trying to make an onion bread, I went off on a tangent and made this potpourri bread. It was a most exhilarating experience. The assortment of ingredients is startling, but the bread turned out rather well—a stick-to-the-rib kind of bread. One of the ingredients used, ground chocolate, had been on my shelf several months, a memento of a quick trip to San Francisco.

In a bowl, crumble 1/2 oz. of fresh yeast in 1/2 cup of warm water. Add 2 tables. vegetable oil, 2 tables. sour cream and 2 tables. grated onion. Cut in 2 tables. of cold margarine with a knife. Add 2 large eggs, 1/2 teas. minced garlic, 2 dashes celery salt, 2 pinches caraway seeds, 2 tables. instant dry skim milk, 2 tables. brown sugar, 3/4 teas. salt, 2 teas. ground chocolate, 1/2 cup creamed cottage cheese, 2 tables. concentrated frozen orange juice and 2 tables. of minced banana. Stir all this together with a spoon. Add 1 3/4 cups whole wheat flour, 4 tables. rye flour, 1 cup unbleached white flour and 4 tables. of wheat germ and stir until mixed. Let rest for 15 minutes.

Turn out mixture onto a white floured board. Use 1 tables. of white flour. Move the dough back and forth. Put 1/4 cup of white flour on top of dough and knead very gently. Dough should be soft. Let rest for 10 minutes.

Oil a 4 1/4 × 8 1/2 × 2″ aluminum foil pan, roll the dough into it and set in a warm area for 30 minutes. Allow the dough to rise to the top of the pan. Preheat oven to 350° and bake for 35 minutes. Then lower the temperature to 325° and bake for 15 minutes more. Test with a wire tester. Cool in the pan then turn out on a wire rack.

Protein Bread

This bread was made in an effort to incorporate protein and nutrients into a bread which would keep me happy but help me lose weight without giving up eating bread. I shaped it to give me small, aesthetically appealing slices.

In a bowl grate the rind of an orange and break in 2 large eggs. Allow 1/2 oz. of fresh yeast to stand in 1/2 cup of warm water. Stir after 5 minutes and add to orange rind. With a slotted spoon beat in 3 teas. honey, 1 teas. salt and 1 cup of instant dry skim milk powder. Blend in 2 1/4 cups of whole wheat flour and stir vigorously for a few minutes. Lastly add 1/2 cup of rye flour and blend.

On a counter top, make a patch of 1/4 cup plus 2 tables. of rye flour and place dough there. Sprinkle some of the rye flour on the top of the dough and start to knead. This should be an extremely sticky dough. I found it necessary to oil the counter to keep the dough from sticking. Knead with some more rye flour, about 1/8 cup until the flour is absorbed. Finish kneading with 1/4 cup wheat germ to give the dough some body. It will still be sticky.

Oil the dough and shape into a sausage-shaped roll, about 12 inches long. Let rise until double in size on an oiled pan 9 × 13 3/4 × 2 1/2". Preheat oven to 350° and bake for 45 minutes until creamy brown. Check with a wire tester. Cool on a rack.

Sesame Seed Bread

Have you ever wandered into a health food store? I recently made a trip to the store for some organic corn meal. How many times have you gone into a supermarket to purchase a few necessities and come out with more than you needed? There was millet seed, carob powder, sesame seed and a variety of interesting items. Curiosity led me to the refrigerator to look at the various health breads. The result of this shopping spree was a wonderful sesame seed bread.

Measure 1 cup of unsweetened pineapple juice in a bowl and dissolve 1/2 oz. of fresh yeast. Stir in and mix thoroughly 1 teas. salt, 1 cup sesame seeds, 3 tables. vegetable oil, 1 tables. honey and 2 cups of unbleached white flour. Let rest for 15 minutes in a warm place.

Gently remove dough from the bowl and place on an oiled 4 1/4 × 8 1/2 × 2" aluminum foil pan. Sprinkle top with 1/2 cup of sesame seeds. Preheat oven to 350° and bake for 45 minutes, until sesame seeds are golden. Check with a wire tester. Remove the bread carefully to a wire rack. Turn right side up.

Yam Bread

The fun of creating bread is to use any ingredients you may have in the house. I defrosted some leftover yams that were in the freezer and had the pleasure of putting them into this bread.

Mix 1 cup of canned yams with 2 tables. of honey. Combine 1/2 oz. fresh yeast, which has been dissolved in 1/2 cup warm water, with 1/2 teas. salt, 1/2 teas. raw sugar, 2 tables. vegetable oil and stir together with 1/2 cup of unbleached white flour. After 10 minutes in a warm place, add this to the yam mixture with 2/3 cup of unbleached white flour and stir.

Flatten the dough on a board sprinkled with some white flour. Break up 4 tables. of margarine with your fingers and spread on the top. Fold dough over and over. Knead, adding 1 1/4 cup of white flour, until the dough is pliable, about 5 minutes, adding more flour if necessary.

Shape into a round loaf and allow to rise until double in an oiled 9 × 13 3/4 × 2 1/2″ pan. Preheat oven to 375° and bake for 40 to 50 minutes. Cool on a rack.

GARLIC BREADS

Crusty Garlic Bread

In a bowl dissolve 1/2 oz. of fresh yeast in 1 cup of warm water. Add 1 teas. salt, 2 tables. vegetable oil and 6 cloves of crushed garlic (use a garlic press). Stir in 3 cups of unbleached white flour and 3 tables. of wheat germ and mix ingredients with a fork.

Make a patch of 1/4 cup of white flour on a board, turn out dough and roll gently back and forth to coat it. Then knead, adding 1/4 cup of white flour gradually for 2 minutes. Let rise until it has doubled on the board. Punch down and let rest for 5 minutes. Scatter some white flour on the board and roll the dough with the hands into a 13-inch length.

Set the bread on an oiled 9 × 13 3/4 × 2 1/2" pan. Oil the surface. Let proof for about 20 minutes. Set oven temperature to 375° and bake for 45 to 55 minutes until light golden. Cool on a rack.

Hearty Garlic Bread

This bread is for those who like the hearty, zestful flavor of garlic—hence, 12 cloves of garlic.

Serve this hearty bread in thick slices spread with butter or margarine with a plate of steaming beans. This is economical and nutritious and offers a goodly portion of the daily quota of protein.

In a deep bowl, dissolve 1/2 oz. of fresh yeast at room temperature into 1 cup of warm water. To this add 3 tables. vegetable oil, 1 teas. salt and 1/4 teas. of raw sugar. Use a slotted spoon to beat in 1 1/2 cups of unbleached white flour and 12 cloves of garlic (use a garlic press to squeeze the garlic through).

Add an additional 1 1/2 cups of flour slowly, working this in from the sides and bottom of the bowl. Now use your fingers to squeeze the dough together.

Bang the dough down hard on the board several times. (This is excellent for pounding out frustrations and also makes the dough easy to handle.)

Form into an oval and set in an oiled 4 1/4 × 8 1/2 × 2″ pan. Oil the surface and let rise in a warm place until a fraction above the top of the pan. Preheat oven at 375° and bake bread for 45 to 55 minutes. Test with a wire tester. Cool right side up on a wire rack.

One Bowl Garlic Bread

In a bowl mix 1/2 oz. fresh yeast, 1 teas. salt, 1 cup warm water, 1/8 cup vegetable oil and 2 large cloves of garlic (use a garlic press to squeeze the garlic through). Beat in 2 cups of unbleached white flour with a slotted spoon for about 20 strokes. Mix in another 1/2 cup of flour.

Blend in the last 1/2 cup of flour with the other ingredients. Bang the dough down several times on the board. Form into an oval bread and set in an oiled 5 1/2 × 9 1/2 × 2 3/4" bread pan.

Allow to rise in a warm place until double. Bake in a preheated 350° oven for 40 to 50 minutes until light golden. Cool on a rack right side up.

Quick Garlic Bread

Garlic was one of the chief vegetables eaten by ancient slaves and laborers. Like many other aromatic herbs, the Greek poets sung its praises. In their agony in Egypt, the Israelites learned to eat garlic, evidently with great enjoyment.

In a bowl mix 1/2 oz. fresh yeast, 1 teas. salt, 3/4 cup warm water and 4 large crushed cloves of garlic (use a garlic press). Now beat in 1 cup of unbleached white flour with a fork. Add 1 cup of white flour and continue beating and stirring the flour. Add another 1/2 cup of white flour, stirring and blending until it forms a cohesive ball. The dough is sticky and soft.

Oil a 3 1/4 × 5 3/4 × 2 1/4" pan. Spoon the dough into it and smooth with oiled fingers. Let rise until it reaches the top of the pan. Preheat oven to 350° and bake for about 1 hour. Check with a wire tester. Cool on a rack.

HERB
AND SPICE
BREADS

Herb Bread

Herbs have been cultivated for centuries for their high food value. Their leaves and stems were commonly used to season foods as early as the 1600s.

In a bowl mash 1/2 oz. of fresh yeast in 1/4 cup of warm water. Keep stirring the following ingredients as you add them to the yeast mixture: 1 1/2 cups unbleached white flour, 1 large egg, 1 pinch oregano, 2 pinches parsley flakes, 3 pinches freeze-dried chopped chives, 2 tables. vegetable oil, 1/4 teas. raw sugar and 1 teas. of salt. Allow to rest for 15 minutes.

Lay the dough on 1/4 cup of white flour. Add more white flour on top, about 1/8 cup, and knead gently. It is a very soft dough. Let rest for 10 minutes. Knead again for a short time with a bit more white flour, about 1 tables.

Fit the dough into an oiled 3 3/4 × 7 1/2 × 2″ aluminum foil pan. Allow to proof for 20 minutes in a warm place. Preheat oven to 350° and bake for 40 to 50 minutes until light brown. Cool in the pan for 5 minutes. Remove to a rack.

High Tor Sesame Twist

This bread is crunchy and chewy. Its appearance is delightful.

In a bowl put 1/2 oz. fresh yeast in 1/2 cup water with 1/2 cup vegetable oil, 1 teas. salt, 1 tables. lemon juice, and 3 tables. of honey. Stir with a fork quite well. Now add 2 1/8 cups of unbleached white flour and mix thoroughly. Add 1/2 cup of white flour. Now use your fingers to mix the ingredients together. Oil the dough and pull like taffy for 5 minutes, until it becomes sticky. Set on a counter surface.

Knead on 1 1/2 tables. of white flour for a short time. Form the dough into an oval. Cut into three even pieces. Roll each piece into a sausage about 10 inches long and braid them together into a twist.

Set on an oiled 9 × 13 3/4 × 2 1/2″ pan. Oil the surface and sprinkle generously with sesame seeds. Allow to rise until quite light, about 25 minutes. Preheat oven to 400° and bake for 30 minutes. Check with a wire tester. Cool.

One Bowl Gingerbread

Marco Polo, during his travels in China in the thirteenth century, wrote glowingly of ginger. Early in the sixteenth century, the Spaniards brought the plants to the New World; and as a result, we still enjoy the superb flavor of ginger which is now grown in Jamaica.

In a bowl dissolve 1/2 oz. of fresh yeast in 1/4 cup of warm skim milk. Make a depression in a mixture of 1 cup of unbleached white flour and 1 cup of whole wheat flour. In its center put 1/2 teas. ginger, 3/4 teas. salt, 1 medium beaten egg, 2 tables. brown sugar, 1 tables. honey, 1/4 cup vegetable oil and the yeast mixture. Mix with a fork; stir the flour to blend and then squeeze with the fingers to form a ball of dough. Oil the dough and shape into a round bread. Allow to double in size on an oiled 8 1/2 × 11 × 1 1/2″ pan.

Preheat oven to 375° and bake for 30 minutes until golden brown. This recipe makes a small loaf and can easily be doubled.

Spice Bread

During the Middle Ages, cloves were used to sweeten and preserve foods. Many fifteenth-century recipes mention cinnamon, cloves and ginger.

Use a large bowl. Sprinkle 1/2 oz. of fresh yeast in 1 cup of strong warm coffee. Add 3/4 cup unbleached white flour, 1 teas. salt, 6 tables. vegetable oil and 1 tables. of honey. Stir in well and set aside for 10 minutes in a warm place. To this mixture add 2 large beaten eggs, 2 cups white flour, 2 cups whole wheat flour, 1/2 teas. ginger, 1/2 teas. cinnamon and 1 teas. of ground cloves. Mix thoroughly. Use your fingers to mix in 1/3 cup dark seedless raisins.

Bounce the dough up and down several times. Shape into a round form and let rise on an oiled 9 × 13 3/4 × 2 1/2″ pan until double in bulk. Preheat oven to 350° and bake for 45 minutes. Check with a wire tester. Cool.

HONEY BREADS

Honey is the worlds oldest natural food—its use for human consumption dates back to ancient times. According to the type of nectar, it varies in flavor, color and composition.

In addition to its flavor-enhancing value, acidity and high sugar content, honey serves to hinder harmful bacterial growth. Baked goods are kept fresh and moist by the use of this product. It is a readily digestable, as well as tasteful, food because the simple sugars that make up the greatest portion of honey require no digestive change before they can be absorbed.

Some medical authorities believe that it has a beneficial influence in the retention of calcium, particularly well suited for infants.

Anne's Sweet Honey
Cake/Bread

In a bowl of an electric mixer dissolve 1/2 oz. of fresh yeast in 1/4 cup of warm coffee. Add 1/2 cup honey, 1 large egg, 1 teas. salt and 1/2 cup of vegetable oil. Beat with the mixer for 1 minute at medium speed. Remove bowl. Add 1 3/4 cups of unbleached white flour and beat again with mixer at a slow speed for 1 minute.

Spoon the dough into an oiled 3 3/4 × 7 1/2 × 2″ pan and set in a warm place until the dough rises to the top of the pan. Preheat oven to 350° and bake for 40 to 50 minutes. Cool in pan for 15 minutes. Invert on a wire rack and turn right side up.

Beehive Honey Bread

In a deep bowl combine 1/2 cup warm water with 1/2 oz. fresh yeast, 3/4 teas. salt, 4 tables. vegetable oil and 6 tables. of honey. Slowly work in 2 1/8 cups of unbleached white flour and beat mixture thoroughly.

Flour the board with 2 1/4 tables. of white flour and knead for about 5 minutes, using just enough flour to keep the dough from sticking. Form into an oval and place in an oiled 3 1/4 × 5 3/4 × 2 1/2″ pan. Use your fingers to spread oil on the surface. Let rise in a warm place until double in size.

Preheat oven to 350° and bake for 45 to 55 minutes. Check with a wire tester. Cool for about 15 minutes and remove carefully to a rack.

Clover Honey Bread

I recently received a lovely present—honey from my friend's own beehive. This bread is tasty spread with cream cheese.

Use an electric mixer. Put 2 large eggs in the bowl with 1/2 cup honey, 1 teas. salt, 1/2 cup vegetable oil, 1/2 oz. soft fresh yeast and 1/2 cup of warm coffee. Beat at medium speed for 2 minutes. Using a wooden spoon, gradually mix in 3 cups of unbleached white flour, 1 cup at a time.

Oil your hands and form bread into an oval shape and fit into an oiled 5 1/2 × 9 1/2 × 2 3/4″ pan. Smooth the surface with oiled fingers. Allow to rise in a warm place until the dough doubles in size.

Preheat oven to 350° and bake for 40 to 50 minutes. Check with a wire tester. Cool on a rack.

Elixir Honey Bread

In a bowl dissolve 1/2 oz. of fresh yeast in 1 cup of warm strong coffee. Mix in 4 tables. unbleached white flour, 1 teas. salt and 5 tables. of vegetable oil. Beat together and set aside for 15 minutes in a warm place. Blend in 1 1/2 cups of white flour and 2 cups of organic whole wheat flour to form a dough.

Sprinkle a little white flour, about 1/8 cup, on a counter surface and set the dough on it. Knead lightly, pressing your fingers into the dough. Turn the dough over and repeat this procedure for a short time.

Form into an oval bread. Set in an oiled aluminum foil pan, 4 1/4 × 8 1/2 × 2″, and let rise until light, about 30 to 35 minutes. Preheat oven to 350° and bake for 1 hour. Check with a wire tester. Cool on a rack.

Honey Yogurt Cake/Bread

In a large bowl dissolve 1/2 oz. fresh yeast in 1/4 cup warm orange juice with a pinch of sugar and salt. Beat in 1/2 cup of unbleached white flour. Remove to a warm area for 15 minutes. Add 1/4 cup vegetable oil, 1/4 cup yogurt, 1 large egg, 1/2 teas. salt, 2 tables. wheat germ, 6 tables. honey and 2 1/4 cups of white flour. Oil your fingers and mix the dough in the bowl.

Form into an oval to fit an oiled 3 3/4 × 7 1/2 × 2″ pan. Oil the top. Allow to rise until double. Preheat oven to 400° and bake for 30 minutes. Cool in the pan for about 15 minutes. Set on a rack. Turn right side up.

Inner Contentment
Honey Bread

In a bowl dissolve 1/2 oz. of fresh yeast in 1/2 cup of warm water. Stir in 4 tables. vegetable oil, 6 tables. honey and 3/4 teas. of salt. Mix in 2 cups of unbleached white flour and beat for 30 strokes to make a dough.

Spread 1/2 cup of white flour on a board and knead, pressing down with the heel of the hands for several minutes. Form into an oval, oil the surface and place in an oiled 3 1/4 × 5 3/4 × 2 1/4″ pan.

Let rise in a warm place until 1 inch above top of pan.

Bake in a preheated 350° oven for 40 to 50 minutes. Test with a wire. Cool in the pan for 10 minutes before removing to a rack. Turn right side up.

Light Honey Bread/Cake

In 1/2 cup of strong warm coffee dissolve 1/2 oz. of fresh yeast. In a bowl mix together 1 1/2 cups of organic whole wheat flour and 1/2 cup of unbleached white flour and make a depression in the center. Pour in the yeast mixture, add 3/4 teas. salt, 6 tables. vegetable oil and 6 tables. of honey. Stir ingredients thoroughly with a slotted spoon and beat for about 20 strokes.

Put 4 tables. of white flour on a board and set the dough on it. Roll back and forth with the hands; then knead lightly until the flour is absorbed. Shape into an oval loaf and set in an oiled pan 3 3/4 × 7 1/2 × 2 1/2". Oil the top of the dough and allow to rise to the top of the pan.

Preheat oven to 350° and bake for 40 to 50 minutes. Cool on a wire rack.

Magic Formula Honey Loaf

In a bowl mix 1/2 cup warm water, 3/4 teas. salt, 1/2 oz. fresh yeast, 4 tables. vegetable oil and 6 tables. of honey. Blend in 2 cups of unbleached white flour and beat vigorously with a slotted spoon for 20 strokes.

Spoon into an oiled 3 1/4 × 5 3/4 × 2" pan, oil surface and smooth with your fingers to even mixture. Let rise until light, about 30 minutes. Preheat oven to 350° and bake about 40 to 50 minutes. Check with a wire tester. Cool in the pan for 10 minutes. Turn out on a rack.

100% Whole Wheat Honey Bread

In a small bowl dissolve 1/2 oz. of fresh yeast in 1/2 cup of warm water. Add 1 teas. salt, 1/4 teas. sugar and 1 cup of stone-ground whole wheat flour. Stir and set aside for about 20 to 30 minutes.

In a large bowl make a well in 3 cups of whole wheat flour. In the center, spoon yeast sponge, 1/4 cup honey, 1 large beaten egg, 1/4 cup vegetable oil and 1/2 cup of warm skim milk. Mix center ingredients with a fork and then beat until thoroughly mixed. Oil your hands and squeeze the dough to form a ball.

Set the dough on 1/8 cup of whole wheat flour on a board and knead for about 5 minutes. Lift and bounce the dough down several times. Place in a bowl, cover with a towel and allow to rise in a warm place (about 25 minutes). Punch down.

On a sprinkling of flour, form into a round loaf. Set on an oiled 5 1/2 × 9 1/2 × 2 3/4" pan. Oil the surface and allow to double. Preheat oven to 350° and bake for about 1 hour. Check with a wire tester. Cool on a rack.

ITALIAN BREADS

I became acquainted with Russ La Scala while patronizing his father's bakery. It was here that I purchased my first Italian whole wheat bread. When young Russ learned of my enthusiasm and interest in bread making, he invited me to see how Italian breads are made.

What a delightful experience it was to see the huge vats of dough, the array of loaves, their different sizes and shapes. Several bakers, including Russ's father, were busy shaping Sicilian breads, which require a special technique. These were made with a heavier dough than the picturesque Calabraise bread, with its round shape and raised points.

I saw them pound round pieces of dough with their fists to remove the air, then fold the dough in half, pound them again and fold in half for their shape. Others were immersed in water and then rolled in sesame seeds. Twisted ones, made of a very flexible dough were rolled into a long form, about 20 inches, and then twisted into figure eights.

At the other end of the bakery was a huge thermostatically controlled, brick-lined steam oven. A tremendous 20-foot twisted loaf was baking inside. A baker stood at the side of the oven with trays of proofed round breads and busily notched designs with a sharp knife. These designs were varied to suit the customers' tastes. I wanted a knife like the one he used for very much the same purpose. It was a Viennese knife and the baker told me where to purchase one.

Mr. La Scala walked with me to the shop at the front of the bakery where he retails his breads. He proudly showed me a 35-year old pamphlet printed by Fleishman's Yeast Company in honor of his father who had been a baker for over 50 years. A photo in the booklet showed his father, one of four generations of bakers, standing in front of his coal-fired oven, holding a long bread paddle. We spoke for a while about those times and I questioned him about the breads. "A baker had to use judgment in those days, to know how to heat the oven with the coals and when to take out the breads. Some people think that the old breads were better, but I disagree."

My next stop was a rather dusty, musty smelling old store to buy the Viennese knife. The store owner, Mr. Raubvogel, told me that they hadn't been manufactured for a good many years. "I have a few minutes to spare and want to tell you about some people who came to my old store on First Avenue, about 30 years ago. One was a rich woman who drove down from Connecticut to buy some pans for baking. She liked to bake for her guests. Do you know who she was?" He hesitated dramatically at this point. "She was Anne Rudin who made the Pepperidge Farm Breads and later sold her company for a fortune. . . . . There was another person who came down in his battered station wagon, Mr. Arnold, to buy supplies for his breads. He made a great success and built up the Arnold Bread Company."

Mr. Raubvogel went over to his desk, rummaged for a while and then handed me an old battered knife. "This is a Viennese knife which I've been using to open my letters." My day was perfect. I hurried home, made my special Italian bread and put my Viennese knife to use.

Quick Pizza Bread

In a bowl soften 1/2 oz. of fresh yeast in 1/2 cup of warm water. Stir in 1 teas. salt, 1 cup unbleached white flour and 1/8 cup of vegetable oil. Set aside in a warm place for about 15 minutes. Use a spoon to mix in the last 1/2 cup of white flour.

On a counter top, make a patch of 1/2 cup of white flour and set the dough on it. Knead until the dough is no longer sticky. Press the dough evenly into an oiled 11″ round pan. Let rest for 15 minutes. Top with your favorite pizza topping. Preheat oven to 375° and bake for 20 to 30 minutes. Serve hot.

No-Knead Italian
Whole Wheat Bread

One morning, I took a trip to Mulberry Street in New York City and made a visit to an Italian bakery. The small round loaf I bought was part of my lunch, with a piece of cheese. I asked the elderly person behind the counter (I assumed she was the baker's wife), "Do you know how this bread is made?" "All I know is you take a sack of flour. . . ."

I measured the bread at home, looked at it, analyzed it and made two breads. The following ingredients are added and then squeezed with the fingers, which is my newest, fast method—a no-knead Italian bread. All other Italian breads are kneaded.

In a bowl dissolve 1/2 oz. fresh yeast in 1 cup water with 1 teas. salt and 2 tables. of vegetable oil. Beat in 1 cup of whole wheat flour. Add another cup of whole wheat flour. Stir, then beat thoroughly. Add the last cup of whole wheat flour plus 2 tables. Start to stir, then use your fingers to squeeze the dough several times so that the ingredients are mixed. On a counter surface, bang the dough down several times.

Shape into a small round bread and set in a 9" round pan sprinkled with corn meal and allow to double. Preheat oven to 375° and bake for 35 to 45 minutes until light golden. Cool on a rack.

Sesame Seed Italian Bread

Make a well in 3 cups of unbleached white flour in a deep bowl. In the hollow stir together 1/2 oz. of fresh yeast with 3/4 cup of warm water. Now add 2 teas. olive oil, 1 teas. salt and 1/4 cup of sesame seeds, mixing the center ingredients slowly at first with a spoon, then stirring together all the flour to make the dough.

On a flat surface, knead with about 1/4 cup of white flour for a few minutes. Bounce the dough several times. Repeat again with 1/4 cup of white flour and knead for a few minutes.

Shape the dough into a roll about 10 inches long, taper the ends. Oil the surface and roll in sesame seeds. Oil a 9 × 13 3/4 × 2 1/2" pan and set the dough in gently. Allow to rise until nearly double in size.

Preheat oven to 375° and bake for 15 minutes, decrease temperature to 350° and bake for 30 minutes more. Cool on a rack.

Special Italian Bread

Italian bread is a perennial favorite. This bread is quick and easy; it rises quite well and is a large, light loaf.

In a bowl dissolve 1/2 oz. of fresh yeast in 1 cup of warm water with 1 1/4 teas. of salt. In a bowl make a hollow in 3 cups unbleached white flour. Pour in the yeast mixture and stir the flour near the center into the yeast mixture, gathering the remainder of the flour to make the dough.

Place on 1/2 cup of white flour on a counter surface. Press the dough into the flour with the tips of the fingers until the flour is enveloped into the dough. Knead for about 5 minutes, with the heels of the hands gradually adding 1/4 cup of white flour.

Roll the dough back and forth to about 15 inches in length. Pat to flatten it. Now fold it into three parts and roll it until it is 16 1/2 inches.

Sprinkle corn meal on a heavy 11 × 16" cookie sheet and set bread on it. Using a sharp knife, make a slit 1 1/2" deep across the bread. Let it rise in a warm 140° oven or a warm area until light. Remove and preheat oven to 375°. Set a pan of hot water in the bottom of the oven and bake the bread for 10 minutes. Reduce the temperature to 350° and bake for about 50 minutes more. Remove to a rack and cool.

Whole Wheat Italian Bread

This bread was served to a group of people whom I had just met for the first time. Someone asked about the type of yeast used. I told her I used fresh yeast which I freeze. This solves the problem of having yeast available when needed. This is a satisfying bread and is fun to make.

In a warm bowl dissolve 1/2 oz. of fresh yeast in 1 cup of warm water. Add 1 teas. salt, 3 tables. vegetable oil and 2 cups of whole wheat flour. Use a slotted spoon to stir for 20 strokes.

On a board, put 1 cup of whole wheat flour and set dough on it. Knead steadily for 5 minutes. You may have to use a little more flour if the dough is too sticky.

Form into a 10-inch oval and oil the surface. Roll it, to narrow the shape and taper the ends. Set on a 9 × 13 3/4 × 2 1/4" pan sprinkled with corn meal. Let double in a warm area. Preheat oven to 350° and bake bread for about 50 minutes. Check with a wire tester. Cool on a rack.

NOSTALGIC
BREADS

Golden Twisted
Sabbath Challah

Nostalgia plays an important role in my creative bread making. I remember my mother baking challah; the heavenly aroma that filled our home has never left my memory. I was fascinated watching my mother kneading and cutting the dough; and I remember putting my nose quite close to it to smell the yeasty odor. She rolled each piece into a heavy rope and then put a weight on at the edge of the four strands before she started to braid them. Four large chicken feathers, which my mother had plucked herself, were tied together at the ends to form a brush. These were dipped in a foamy mixture of egg and water and spread on the challah.

This golden twisted loaf graced our Sabbath table and was placed on a snowy white linen tablecloth and was flanked by two silver candelabra. This twisted challah is my special effort to bring to fruition that special time in my life.

Make a yeast sponge in a small bowl by dissolving 1/2 oz. of fresh yeast in 1/2 cup of warm water. Add 1 teas. of salt and 2 tables. of raw sugar. Beat in 1 cup of unbleached white flour with a slotted spoon for a minute. Set in a warm place to proof for 20 minutes. Mix 1 large egg with 2 tables. of raw sugar and set in heated water to simmer gently until the sugar is dissolved. Remove from heat and cool.

In a bowl make a well in 2 1/2 cups of unbleached white flour. In the center break in 2 large eggs, then add 1/4 cup of vegetable oil, yeast sponge and egg mixture. Use a slotted spoon to stir these ingredients in well.

Spread 1/2 cup of white flour on a board and lay dough down and knead for 5 minutes until the dough is smooth. Divide dough into three parts. Then on a lightly floured board, roll each one into a heavy rope about 8 inches long and braid them together, tucking the ends under.

Set on an oiled 9 × 13 3/4 × 2 1/2″ pan. Spread the sides and the top with part of a beaten egg. Sprinkle the top with poppy seeds. Let rise in a warm area for about 30 minutes.

Preheat oven to 400° and bake challah for 20 minutes. Lower temperature to 350° and continue baking for 30 to 40 minutes more. Check with a wire tester. Remove to a wire rack.

Light Challah

This challah is sure to be a favorite, for it is a new, fast method which doesn't require two risings. It has a light, porous texture.

In a deep bowl, crumble 1/2 oz. of fresh yeast in 1/2 cup of warm water. Add 1/2 cup vegetable oil, 1 teas. salt, grated rind of a small lemon and 3 tables. of honey. Put in 1 1/2 cups of unbleached white flour and beat with a slotted spoon. Break in 2 large eggs and beat well with the spoon. Add an additional 1 cup of white flour and blend it well with the other ingredients.

Set the dough on a flat surface. Knead, gradually adding 1/2 cup of white flour until all the flour is absorbed. Add 1/4 cup more of white flour and knead until the dough is slightly sticky. Pull like taffy for several minutes. Give the dough a final light kneading with 1/4 cup of white flour, folding it several times as you knead it. Turn it round and round into a ball. Divide the dough into three pieces. Roll each one on a sprinkling of white flour until about 10 inches long. Braid these rolls and tuck the ends under.

Oil a pan, 9 × 13 3/4 × 2 1/2", and set the challah in the center. Spread the top and the sides with beaten egg and then sprinkle the top with poppy seeds. Allow to rise until double in size. If you want a high challah, put it in a small pan, allowing 1 to 1 1/2 inches on all sides for rising. For a longer challah, equally as good, set in a longer pan.

Preheat oven to 400° and bake 30 to 40 minutes until a golden brown. Check with a wire tester. Cool on a rack.

Mama's Coffee Cake/Bread

In a bowl dissolve 1/2 oz. fresh yeast in 1/4 cup warm water with 1/4 teas. salt and 1/4 teas. of raw sugar. Beat in 1/2 cup of unbleached white flour. Set aside where it is warm for 10 minutes. Add 1/3 cup dark seedless raisins, 1 tables. wheat germ, 1/4 cup yogurt (Mama used sour cream), 4 1/2 tables. honey, 1/2 teas. salt and 1 large beaten egg. Beat vigorously with a fork. Add 1 1/2 cups of unbleached white flour and stir to form the dough.

Make a patch with 1/2 cup of white flour on a counter surface; set the dough on it. Press the dough into the flour with your fingers, turning it over and repeating until all the flour is absorbed into the dough.

Shape into a round loaf, oil the surface and place in an oiled 3 3/4 × 5 3/4 × 2 1/4" pan. Let rise until double in size. Preheat oven to 400° and bake for 30 minutes until brown. Turn out on a wire rack. Set right side up. This recipe can easily be doubled; use an aluminum foil pan 4 1/4 × 8 1/2 × 2".

Milk and Honey Bread

This recipe is a childhood joy relived. Reading John Greenleaf Whittier's *The Barefoot Boy,* I came upon a line referring to the pleasures of eating bread and milk. When my sister, Mary, and I were young girls, our supper sometimes consisted of home baked challah (a Jewish bread) and milk. I remember sitting, in the warmth of our home, at the kitchen table, slowly putting pieces of challah into a glass, adding sugar and my mother pouring hot milk into it to soften the bread. The mound of bread grew and swelled from the hot milk. It was fun to invert the glass into a round bowl and to enjoy the sight of a hill of goodies. I found after reading this poem that the joys of childhood can be relived and I recently savored this challah with as much enthusiasm as I had when I was a small child. I made this bread as close as possible to my mother's original recipe.

In a small bowl mix 1/2 oz. fresh yeast in 1/2 cup warm water with 1 teas. salt, 1 teas. sugar and 3 tables. of vegetable oil. Add 1 1/2 cups of unbleached white flour to the yeast mixture. Set aside in a warm spot to become light, about 30 minutes. In a large bowl make a well in 2 1/4 cups of white flour. In the center add the yeast sponge and 1 large beaten egg. Stir this mixture with 1/2 cup of warm water to form the dough.

Remove from the bowl to a flat surface and add 1/4 cup of white flour, pressing this into the dough with the fingers. Bang the dough up and down to make a cohesive ball. Cut the dough into three even parts. Turn each one round and round with the palms and set close together on an oiled 9 × 13 3/4 × 2 1/2″ pan.

Spread the surface with some beaten egg and let rise where it is warm for about 30 minutes. Preheat oven to 375° and bake for 45 to 55 minutes. Cool on a rack.

Orange Twirl Challah

The spiral shape used for this challah is a good omen, the continuation of good health for the year round.

In a bowl measure 1/2 cup warm water and add 1/2 oz. soft fresh yeast, 1/4 cup vegetable oil, grated rind of an orange, 3 tables. honey, 2 large eggs and 1 teas. of salt. Beat with a slotted spoon for a few minutes. Add 2 cups of unbleached white flour, 1 cup at a time, and stir the mixture slowly at first, then beat until smooth. Mix in 1 1/4 cups of white flour and stir. Add another 1/2 cup of white flour and use the side of the spoon to mix the ingredients together.

Oil a counter surface and set the dough on it. Oil your fingers and press into the dough to further mix it. Now pull like taffy for about 5 minutes. Bounce the dough down hard several times.

Knead for a few minutes with 1 tables. of white flour until the dough is smooth. Form into a roll about 15 inches long and wind it round and round like a beehive, tucking the top end into the center.

Set on an oiled 9 × 13 3/4 × 2 1/2″ pan. Spread surface with part of a beaten egg. Let rise in a warm area, about 25 minutes. Preheat oven to 400° and bake for 15 minutes; lower temperature to 350° and bake for 30 to 40 minutes. Cool on a rack.

Scallion Bread

Scallions were used by my mother in a special goodie. It was a mixture of pot cheese, eggs and fried minced scallions which she encased in her own fragrant dough. These came out of the oven gloriously golden on the outside and succulent inside. I remember at times she put these into a pot with a lid; and to keep them warm, enfolded the covered pot in a large pillow.

Sauté 1/4 cup of minced scallions in 3 tables. of butter. Cool. In a bowl dissolve 1/2 oz. of fresh yeast in 1/2 cup of warm water. Add 1 teas. salt, 3 tables. raw sugar, 1 large beaten egg and 3 tables. of vegetable oil and stir. Blend in 2 cups of unbleached white flour and set aside in a warm place for about 20 to 30 minutes, until the mixture is light. Stir in the scallions.

Put the dough on 1/2 cup plus 2 1/2 tables. of white flour on a counter surface and knead until soft, about 1 minute. Oil your fingers and form into an oval. Set on an oiled 8 1/2 × 11 × 1 1/2″ pan and allow to double. Preheat oven to 350° and bake for 45 to 55 minutes. Cool on a rack.

Sunset Bread

In a large warm bowl mix and beat together 1/4 cup warm water, 1/2 oz. fresh yeast, 1 teas. salt, 2 large beaten eggs, 1/3 cup vegetable oil, 4 tables. honey and 1 teas. of lemon juice. Beat in 2 cups of unbleached white flour and add another cup of white flour gradually and blend together.

On a counter surface, make a patch of 1/2 cup of white flour and set dough on it. Knead gently for about 3 minutes. This is a soft dough. Give dough a final sprinkling with flour and shape into an oval bread.

Set on an oiled 9 × 13 3/4 × 2 1/2″ pan and brush with part of a well beaten egg. Allow to rise until light, about 30 minutes. You will find that it spreads.

Preheat oven to 400° and bake for 30 minutes. Cool. The finished bread is a cross between a cake and a bread and is most delectable.

PEANUT
BUTTER
BREADS

Crunchy Peanut Bread

Pound for pound, peanuts have more minerals, vitamins and proteins than beef liver. It is a concentrated food with more food energy than sugar. This information may surprise many; the peanut is a pea, not a nut and is a member of the bean family.

This bread is a wholesome, crunchy delight for children.

Grind fresh roasted peanuts. Measure 1 cup, put aside. In a bowl measure 1 cup of warm water, add 1/2 oz. of fresh yeast and stir. Add 8 teas. instant dry skim milk, 1 teas. salt, 2 tables. plus 2 teas. of honey and mix. Now add 3 cups of whole wheat flour, 1/2 cup at a time and stir well. Oil hands and mix in peanuts.

Spoon this mixture into an oiled 3 3/4 × 7 1/2 × 2″ pan. Moisten your fingers with some vegetable oil and smooth the surface. Set the pan in a cold oven, turn temperature to 325° and bake for 1 hour and 15 minutes. Check with a wire tester. Cool on a rack.

Honey Peanut Bread

In a bowl dissolve 1/2 oz. of fresh yeast in 1/2 cup of warm water. Add 3/4 teas. salt, 1/4 cup honey, 1/4 cup instant dry skim milk and 1/2 cup of coarsely ground fresh peanuts. Blend. Then beat in 1 cup of whole wheat flour with a spoon until smooth. Continue beating while adding 1 more cup of whole wheat flour until dough is thoroughly mixed.

On a board, use a minute amount of unbleached white flour, about 1 tables., and turn out dough. Roll it back and forth gently. Fit dough into an oiled 3 1/4 × 5 3/4 × 2 1/4" pan. Oil top and smooth with your fingers to even the surface. Let rise to the top of the pan in a warm area.

Preheat oven to 350° and bake for about 45 minutes. Test with a wire. Cool on a rack. This recipe can easily be doubled and baked in a 3 3/4 × 7 1/2 × 2" pan.

Organic Peanut Butter Bread

In a bowl dissolve 1/2 oz. of fresh yeast in 1/2 cup of warm water. Now add 1 teas. salt, 2 large beaten eggs, 2 tables. honey, 3 tables. vegetable oil and 6 tables. of peanut butter. Beat this well with a fork. Stir in 2 1/4 cups of unbleached white flour and then beat vigorously with a slotted spoon for 20 strokes.

Oil a counter surface and spoon out dough. Add about 1/2 cup of white flour and knead gently for about 2 minutes. Dough should be soft. Form into a round bread and oil the top.

Set in an oiled 8 1/2 × 11 × 1 1/2" pan and set aside for 25 minutes in a warm area. Draw the bread together into a higher round shape just before setting it in the oven. Preheat oven to 375° and bake for 40 minutes. Cool on a rack.

Pippin Peanut Butter Bread

In a bowl stir 1/2 oz. of fresh yeast in 1/2 cup of warm skim milk. With a spoon beat in 1/2 teas. salt, 1 teas. brown sugar and 1 cup of stone-ground whole wheat flour. Set aside to rise in a warm place. Then add the following ingredients and stir thoroughly until well mixed: 1 1/2 cups unbleached white flour, 2 large beaten eggs, 2 tables. vegetable oil and 6 tables. of natural peanut butter.

Spoon out dough on 1/2 cup of white flour on a counter surface. Use a knife to mix in the flour at first, then press with your fingers into the dough, mixing the flour into it. Use the heel of your hands to knead for about 1 minute. Fold the dough in thirds lengthwise, tuck ends under and lay in an oiled aluminum foil pan 4 1/4 × 8 1/2 × 2″. Allow to increase in size until double in bulk.

Preheat oven to 350° and bake the bread for 45 minutes or until done. Use a wire tester. Cool on a rack.

PUMPERNICKEL
BREADS

Caraway
Pumpernickel Bread

In a large bowl dissolve 1/2 oz. of fresh yeast in 1 cup of warm water. Add 2 cups stone-ground whole wheat flour, 4 tables. cider vinegar, 1/4 teas. raw sugar, 1 teas. salt and 2 teas. of caraway seeds. Stir vigorously. Now add 2 cups of whole rye flour and mix together with a wooden spoon to form a dough. Use your fingers to further mix the dough.

Sprinkle some white flour on a counter surface, about 1/8 cup, and knead the dough for about 5 minutes, adding flour only to keep the dough from sticking.

Form into a round bread and set in a 9" round pan. Allow to rise until it has doubled in size. Preheat oven to 350° and bake for 45 minutes to 1 hour. Check with a wire tester. Cool on a rack.

Laya Pumpernickel Bread

This is my favorite pumpernickel bread. I truly enjoy this at breakfast with a small piece of farmer cheese and a strong cup of coffee.

Measure 1/2 cup of warm water in a bowl and dissolve 1/2 oz. of fresh yeast. Drop in 1 large egg. Add 1/4 teas. sugar, 1 teas. salt and 2 tables. of vegetable oil and stir. Beat in 1 cup of whole rye flour and then add 3/4 cup of stone-ground whole wheat flour.

On a dough board put 1/4 cup of whole wheat flour and set dough there. Then sprinkle some rye flour on top of the dough and knead. Add some rye flour, about 1/8 cup, and some whole wheat flour, also about 1/8 cup, and knead for a short time, until the dough becomes sticky. Lift and bounce the dough down hard 10 times. Finish kneading lightly with 1/4 cup of white flour until the dough is slightly sticky.

Shape into a round bread and oil the dough. Now use cider vinegar to cover the entire bread. Set on an oiled 9 × 13 3/4 × 2 1/2″ pan and allow to double. Preheat oven to 350° and bake for 1 hour and 15 minutes. Cool on a rack.

Sidney's Pumpernickel Bread

I love to gather bread anecdotes—for I am always on a busman's holiday away from home. This anecdote is about Sidney, a rolly-polly, balding, loving grandfather, salt-of-the-earth type. Thank the Lord there are still many like him. He was born in a small town in Russia over 50 years ago. He worked very hard at an early age, which was common in that milieu.

When he was about 8 years old, his lot in life was to get up before dawn to help his father, a baker. He could barely reach the huge vat of heavy dough; and one time while standing on a chair, he nearly toppled into the dough.

He described the mill where his father bought flour. At times when the miller couldn't deliver the sacks of flour, his father had to carry them home on his back, one at a time for many miles. The very dark and coarse bread was the mainstay of the diet in that poor community.

In a deep bowl, crumble 1/2 oz. of fresh yeast and stir in 1 cup of warm water and mix with a fork. Beat in 2 cups whole wheat flour, 4 tables. vinegar, 1/2 teas. raw sugar and 1 teas. of salt. Use a wooden spoon to further mix in 2 cups of rye flour. Now use the tip to pound the dough for a short time. Finally, squeeze the dough with the fingers to further mix it.

Spread 1 tables. of whole wheat flour on a board, set the dough there and knead for 5 minutes. Add a bit more flour under the dough so that it is easy to roll back and forth.

Oil the dough and form into a slightly oval shape and set in an oiled 9" round pan. Allow to rise until double and bake in a preheated 400° oven for 45 minutes. Test with a wire tester and tap the bottom of the bread for a hollow sound. Cool on a rack. This yields a one pound loaf and can easily be doubled.

Sour Pumpernickel Bread

Use a deep bowl and mix together 1 cup of unbleached white flour and 1 cup of whole wheat flour. In the center dissolve 1/2 oz. of fresh yeast with 1 1/4 cups of warm water. Then add 6 tables. cider vinegar, 1 teas. salt and 1/4 teas. of sugar and stir. Set aside in a warm place until light, about 30 minutes. Add 2 cups of whole rye flour gradually. Oil your hands and knead the dough in the bowl.

Sprinkle 5 tables. of whole wheat flour on a counter surface. Set the dough on this and knead lightly for a short time.

Shape into a round bread. Oil the surface of the dough. Place in an oiled 9" round pan and allow to double in bulk. Preheat oven to 350° and bake bread for 1 hour until honey brown. Check with a wire tester. Cool on a rack.

RYE BREADS

Chana's Rye Bread

The Chana rye bread and the company rye bread which follow were made with different methods. Each rises well and very quickly. The Chana rye is a tasty bread which I like to serve with cheese; it looks attractive when sliced thick for the cheese tray. Although it takes longer to make, the company bread is bound to bring admiration from your guests.

In a large bowl mix 1/2 cup warm water with 1/2 oz. fresh yeast, 1 tables. cider vinegar, 1 teas. salt, 1/4 teas. raw sugar and 1 teas. of caraway seeds. Then add 1/2 cup white unbleached flour, 1/2 cup whole wheat flour and 1/2 cup of rye flour and stir thoroughly with a spoon.

On a counter surface set the dough on a patch of 1/2 cup of white flour and then dredge top with some whole wheat flour. Lift the mixture over and under to coat the dough and knead until the flour is absorbed. Lift the dough and bounce down on the board about 15 times.

Oil the top and sprinkle with some white flour and turn round and round for a good form. I have discovered that oiling the dough makes a special crust which is delightfully crispy. Place the bread in an oiled 9 × 13 3/4 × 2 1/2" pan. Allow to rise until light, about 25 minutes.

Preheat oven to 350° and bake for 30 minutes. Oil the top again and continue to bake for another 40 minutes until golden in color. Cool on a rack.

Company Rye Bread

I gave this bread to my former employer who felt that it was excellent. He told me the next morning that his young son ate five slices at one sitting. "My wife would like to know what you put into it?" After I gave him a rundown of the ingredients, he said, "No wonder I feel so healthy today."

Measure 1/2 cup warm water in a bowl, add 2 teas. caraway seeds, 1/2 teas. raw sugar, 1/2 oz. fresh yeast, 4 tables. cider vinegar and 1 teas. of salt. Stir well. In a bowl blend together 3/4 cup unbleached white flour, 1/2 cup rye flour and 1/2 cup of whole wheat flour. Pour in the yeast mixture and keep stirring until all the flour is blended.

On a flat surface put 1/4 cup of white flour and place the dough there. Turn the dough over and over with a knife. Knead for 5 minutes, using your fingers to press the flour into the dough. Add 1/8 cup of white flour and knead, again using your fingers to press the flour into the dough. Now using the heel of your hands, add about 1/8 cup of white flour and knead until the dough is less sticky. Bounce the dough down hard 10 times. Roll the dough round and round with both hands.

Oil the top and set into an oiled 3 1/4 × 5 3/4 × 2" pan. Allow to rise until nicely rounded. Bake in a preheated 350° oven for about 30 minutes, oil the top of the bread again and continue to bake until it is a delightful brown color, about 40 minutes more. Cool on a rack.

Crusty Rye Bread

In a deep bowl make a depression in 2 cups of rye flour. In its center blend 1/2 oz. fresh yeast with 1/2 cup warm water, 1 teas. salt, 2 tables. vegetable oil and 2 tables. of cider vinegar. Stir vigorously. Now add 1/2 cup of unbleached white flour and start kneading in the bowl. Press the flour into the dough to give it some body. Add another 1/8 cup of white flour gradually and knead the dough until it is pliable.

Form into a round bread. Use a brush to oil the surface and set in an oiled 9″ round pan. Allow to increase until double. Preheat oven to 350° and bake for 1 hour and 15 minutes. Use a wire tester. Cool on a wire rack.

Caraway Sour Rye Bread

In a deep bowl crumble 1/2 oz. of fresh yeast and stir together with 1 cup of warm water. Add 1 1/4 teas. salt, 3 tables. vegetable oil, 1 tables. caraway seeds and 3 tables. of vinegar. Beat and stir in 3 cups of rye flour, 1 cup at a time.

Turn out on a surface floured with 1/4 cup of rye flour and knead for approximately 5 minutes. Keep adding flour gradually, about 1/4 cup, so dough is slightly sticky.

Form into a round bread and set in an oiled 9″ round pan until it has doubled in volume. Slash top of loaf 1/2-inch deep lengthwise, after it has risen. Bake in a preheated 350° oven for 1 hour to 1 hour and 15 minutes. Check with a wire tester. Cool on a rack.

New England Raisin Rye Bread

One day at dusk, I was out for a walk along the shoreline in Larchmont, New York. The beauty of this area and its ever-changing skyline as it merges with the water has enthralled me many times.

By sheer chance, I came across several men who were waiting at the water's edge to take sightings of the stars and planets. The instructor told me this was a private course in marine navigation. Soon it was dark enough and I had the wonderful experience of seeing Mars, which they pointed out to me.

A young bystander also watching the proceedings told me about his experiences as a midshipman. I told him about my bread making. He mentioned his liking for a raisin rye bread which he purchases regularly in a small town near South Arlington, Massachusetts, where he skis. This bread is the mainstay of his diet.

In a large bowl dissolve 1 oz. of fresh yeast in 2 cups of warm water. Add 6 tables. vegetable oil, 2 teas. salt, 6 tables. cider vinegar and 2 large beaten eggs. Beat with a fork. Mix in 2 cups of stone-ground rye flour and 2 cups of unbleached white flour, then beat thoroughly with a slotted spoon for 25 strokes. Blend in 1/2 cup of dark seedless raisins. Add 2 1/2 cups of whole wheat flour, 1 1/4 cups at a time, and then use your fingers to mix the ingredients together.

On a counter surface, make a patch of 1 cup of unbleached white flour. Turn out the dough and knead until it is slightly sticky. Oil the surface and shape into a round bread. Place on an oiled 9 × 13 3/4 × 2 1/2" pan or cookie sheet and allow to double.

Preheat oven to 350° and bake for about 1 1/2 hours. Check with a wire tester. Cool on a rack.

SNACK BREADS

Butter Buns

Use a bowl to dissolve 1/2 oz. of fresh yeast in 1/2 cup of warm water. Add 1/8 cup vegetable oil, 1 large beaten egg and 1/2 teas. of salt. Beat thoroughly. Gradually beat in 2 1/4 cups of unbleached white flour until the dough is soft.

Separate twelve pieces of dough and form into round buns on a counter surface. Place on an oiled 9 × 13 3/4 × 2 1/2" pan. Allow to increase in size. Spread tops with 4 tables. of melted sweet butter. Set aside in a warm area for 20 minutes.

Set oven at 200° and bake for 15 minutes. Increase temperature to 350° and bake until a rich golden brown, about 20 minutes. Cool on a rack.

Cream Cheese Rolls

In a bowl, crumble 1/2 oz. of fresh yeast in 1/2 cup of warm skim milk and mix. Combine 2 cups whole wheat flour, 3 tables. honey, 1 teas. salt, 5 tables. soft cream cheese and 2 tables. of soft margarine with the first mixture.

Spread 1/2 cup of unbleached white flour on a bread board, set the dough there and knead for 2 minutes; dough will be slightly sticky. Allow it to double in bulk on the board. Form into eight round rolls and set on an oiled cookie sheet 11 × 16", allowing space between each for spreading.

Preheat oven to 375° and bake for 20 to 30 minutes. Check with a wire tester. Cool on a rack.

Crescent Finger Rolls

This recipe evolved by sheer luck. After a disappointing experience as the result of the excessive heat in my kitchen, I tried using cold margarine which I cut and pounded into the batter with a knife. The crescents turned out perfectly lovely and flaky.

In a bowl stir 1/2 oz. of fresh yeast with 1/2 cup of warm water and dissolve. Beat in 1 cup of unbleached white flour with a fork. Add 4 tables. margarine (cold), 1 teas. salt and 1 cup of white flour. Use the edge of a knife to cut and pound in the margarine and to mix the ingredients.

Put 1/4 cup of white flour on a bread board, set the dough there and use the fingers to mix the dough with the flour. Let rest for 20 minutes. Separate the dough into twelve pieces. Roll each piece into a 3 inch strand and then shape into a crescent. Set on an oiled cookie sheet 11 × 16" long.

Preheat oven to 375° and bake on the center rack for 20 to 25 minutes. Crescents should be a light, creamy tan color. Cool on a rack.

Parmesan Biscuits

In a bowl make a well in 4 cups of unbleached white flour. In the hollow dissolve 1/2 oz. fresh yeast in 1 cup warm skim milk with 1 teas. of salt. Add 1/4 lb. of soft margarine (cut in small pieces) and mix all the ingredients with a fork, gathering the flour to make a dough. Now oil your fingers and work the margarine through the flour mixture. Turn out on a board. Cut into eight pieces. Form into large round biscuits and set.on an oiled pan 9 × 13 3/4 × 2 1/2″ and let rise in a warm place until double.

Preheat oven to 350° and bake for 20 minutes. Remove from oven, cool for 5 minutes and split the biscuits. Sprinkle bottom halves with 1/2 cup of grated Parmesan cheese. Oil the tops, set on the bottom halves and return to the oven to bake for another 10 to 15 minutes until light brown. Cool on a rack.

Poppy Seed Board

You'll like this one so much, you'll want to double the recipe the next time.

Melt 1/4 lb. of margarine. Measure in a large bowl 1 cup of warm water and stir in 1/2 oz. of fresh yeast. Add 1 1/2 cups unbleached white flour, the melted margarine, 1 teas. salt and 3 tables. of wheat germ. Mix thoroughly and allow to rise in a warm place until light. Blend in 1 1/2 cups of flour. Knead the dough in the bowl with the heel of your hands, folding it back on itself. Repeat this procedure two more times.

Pat the dough to fit a heavily oiled cookie sheet 11 × 16" long. Oil the surface with a brush and sprinkle with 1/2 cup of poppy seeds. Allow to rise in a warm place until almost double.

Preheat oven to 400° and bake for about 30 minutes until light golden. Turn out to cool.

Poppy Seed Rolls

This recipe calls for a happy approach to baking, exercising your fingers and making attractive, appealing rolls.

In a large bowl dissolve 1/2 oz. of fresh yeast in 1/2 cup of warm water. Add 1/2 teas. of salt and 2 tables. of olive oil and stir thoroughly. Now stir in 1 cup of unbleached white flour. Blend in 3/4 cup of flour gradually until the ingredients are thoroughly mixed together. Oil your fingers and work the dough through in the bowl by squeezing with your fingers. Do this several times.

Put about 1/2 cup of flour on a dough board and knead for about 10 minutes for a slightly sticky dough. Cut off 6 pieces of dough and on a sprinkling of white flour roll each into 4-inch strands. Twist these round and round to make snail-like rolls. Use a brush to spread some vegetable oil in a pan and set the rolls with space between them to increase in volume. Coat the rolls lightly with vegetable oil and part of a well beaten egg. Sprinkle the tops with poppy seeds.

Allow to rise in a warm place. Bake in a preheated 350° oven until light golden, about 30 minutes. Cool on a rack.

Rolled Rye Bread

"Waste not, want not," is a good proverb. I had never tried rolled rye cereal and it was on sale in a health food store. I decided to make a bread with the leftover cereal. I found a small piece very satisfying; and with fruit and wine, it's a gourmet's delight.

In a bowl dissolve 1/2 oz. of fresh yeast in 1/2 cup of warm water. Beat in 2 large eggs, 1 tables. honey, 2 tables. instant dry milk, 1/2 cup wheat germ and 1/2 cup of warm skim milk. Stir in vigorously 1 cup of rolled rye cereal. Blend in 2 cups of unbleached white flour.

Spoon dough into an oiled 2 × 8 1/2 × 4 1/4" pan and allow the dough to rise to the top of the pan. Preheat oven to 350° and bake for about 40 to 50 minutes. Check with a wire tester. Cool in the pan for 20 minutes. Turn out on a wire rack.

Rolly Pop
English Muffins

This is a simple, light muffin; a happy blend of unbleached white flour and stone-ground whole wheat flour; and a joy to make. Its texture is light and porous. It was developed to give the family an excellent, healthful muffin. This recipe can be easily doubled.

In a bowl measure 1 cup warm water and stir in 1/2 oz. fresh yeast, 2 tables. vegetable oil and 1 teas. of salt. Beat in 2 cups of unbleached white flour. Now stir in 1 cup of stone-ground whole wheat flour and mix well. Oil the surface of the dough and allow to proof until light, about 25 minutes.

On a counter surface, sprinkle 1/8 cup plus 1 teas. of white flour and set dough there. Knead lightly until soft. Cut dough into six pieces and roll each one in corn meal. Form round muffins 3 3/4" in diameter. Sprinkle a 9 × 13 3/4 × 2 1/2" pan with corn meal and set the muffins there. Flatten slightly.

Preheat oven to 350° and bake for at least 15 minutes. Check with a wire tester. Cool. Separate for toasting, using a fork first and then your fingers.

Whole Wheat Bread Sticks

In a bowl dissolve 1/2 oz. of fresh yeast in 1/4 cup of warm water. Add 1/2 teas. unsulphured molasses, 1 large egg and 1 teas. of salt and mix. Beat in thoroughly 1 cup of unbleached white flour. Gradually blend in 3/4 cup of whole wheat flour, or just enough to make a soft dough.

Spread 1/4 cup of white flour on a counter surface, set dough on it. Knead lightly until the flour is incorporated in the dough. Toss up and down several times.

Pinch off twelve pieces to form bread sticks, rolling each one into a cylindrical form. Set bread sticks apart on an oiled 9 × 13 3/4 × 2 1/2″ pan and let rise for 20 minutes. Preheat oven to 350° and bake for 20 minutes until done. Cool on a rack. You can easily double this recipe.

Whole Wheat Pitta

This bread is unique since it is baked under the gas broiler in the stove. It is a flat bread about 1/4" thick. There are still people who bake bread in large quantities. One such family comes from India; they make a bread which they call *Pitta*. It rises for several hours and is started with a piece of leftover dough used for leavening. The father of this household lives solely on the foods of the Bible. This whole wheat flat bread is a quick version and is made with fresh yeast. Break it into pieces, and keep crisp in a tin can. Serve with a soft cheese spread.

In a bowl dissolve 1/2 oz. fresh yeast in 1 cup warm water with 1 teas. salt and 1/8 cup of vegetable oil. Beat in thoroughly 2 cups of stone-ground whole wheat flour.

On a counter, put 3 generous tables. of unbleached white flour. Set the dough there, and press the fingers into the dough, turning it over and over until the flour has been worked in.

Oil a 13 × 13 3/4" broiler pan. Fit the dough into the pan by using your fingers to press the dough and then pound gently with the fists. Preheat oven to 200° and bake on the lowest rack for approximately 20 minutes on each side until light brown. Allow to cool on a rack.

SOUR DOUGH
BREADS

San Francisco is the home of sour dough bread. Several months ago I took a trip there. My first experience was a visit to a bakery to buy a crusty loaf of sour dough bread, which I joyfully munched as I strolled along Fisherman's Wharf.

The early miners, known as "the forty-niners," were called "sour doughs" for their method of using some left-over dough which they soured and fermented to start a new batch of bread.

Happiness Sour
Dough Bread

In a bowl dissolve 1/2 oz. of fresh yeast in 1 cup of warm water. Add 2 large beaten eggs, 3 tables. cider vinegar and 1 1/4 teas. of salt. Now add 2 cups of unbleached white flour; first stir, then beat until well blended.

On a counter surface make a patch of 1 cup of white flour and set the dough on it. Turn dough over and over to coat it with the flour; then use your fingers to knead lightly till the flour is absorbed. Add 1/2 cup of white flour and knead lightly for 2 minutes.

Form into an oval and oil the top. Put into an oiled aluminum foil pan 4 1/4 × 8 1/2 × 2" and allow to double. Preheat oven to 350° and bake for 40 to 50 minutes. Check with a wire tester. Cool on a rack.

Quick Sour Dough Bread

In a bowl dissolve 1/2 oz. fresh yeast in 1/4 cup warm water with 1 large egg, 1 teas. salt and 2 tables. of cider vinegar. Blend in 1 1/2 cups of unbleached white flour and stir to form the dough.

Turn out on 1 cup of white flour on a board and knead lightly for 5 minutes. The dough should be soft.

Shape into a 7" round bread and set in an oiled 9" round pan. Allow to double in size.

Preheat oven to 350° and bake bread for 1 hour. Check with a wire tester. Cool on a rack.

San Francisco
Sour Dough Bread

In a bowl measure 1 cup of warm water and dissolve 1/2 oz. of fresh yeast. Add 1/4 teas. raw sugar, 1 teas. salt, 4 1/2 tables. cider vinegar and 2 cups of unbleached white flour. Stir and beat this in well. Mix in 2 cups of white flour. After stirring for a short time, you will find it easier to use your fingers to squeeze the dough together. Do this about 10 times; it helps to make a cohesive ball of dough.

Form into an oval loaf and let rise in an oiled pan 9 × 13 3/4 × 2 1/2″ until double. Preheat oven to 350° and bake for 1 hour. Check with a wire tester. Cool on a rack.

SPECIAL
WHITE
BREADS

Country White Bread

This is an enjoyable bread, ideal for a late Sunday family breakfast. It is excellent served with plum jam.

In a bowl dissolve 1/2 oz. of fresh yeast in 1/2 cup of warm water. With a fork, beat in 2 large eggs, 6 tables. instant dry skim milk, 1 teas. salt, 2 tables. honey, 4 tables. vegetable oil and 4 tables. of cold margarine cut into small pieces. Blend in 2 cups of unbleached white flour. Add 2 more cups of white flour.

Knead for a few minutes on a lightly floured board until sticky. Shape into an oval loaf, set in an oiled 4 1/4 × 8 1/2 × 2" pan and even out the mixture with oiled fingers. Let rise to 1 inch above the pan.

Preheat oven to 350° and bake 45 to 60 minutes until golden brown. Test with a wire tester. Cool on a wire rack.

Fragrant White Bread

Measure 3/4 cup of warm skim milk, pour into a bowl and crumble 1/2 oz. of fresh yeast. Add 1 teas. of salt and 1 teas. of honey and stir. Use a spoon to mix in 1 1/2 cups of unbleached white flour. Set in a warm place to rise about 20 to 30 minutes.

Spread 1 cup of white flour on a flat surface. Use the spoon to turn out the dough; mix it with the flour. Knead lightly for a few minutes. Gradually add 1/2 cup of white flour and knead about 5 minutes for a fairly stiff dough.

Form into an oval to fit an oiled 4 1/4 × 8 1/2 × 2" pan. Let rise until double and bake in a 350° preheated oven approximately 1 hour. Check with a wire tester. Cool on a rack.

Snow Ball Bread

This is the first in a series of white breads. I've found bread making an ongoing pursuit; and, as in all creative attainments, one leads to another. This bread should be kneaded by the master of the household since it requires some muscle. It is a closely textured bread.

Measure 1 cup of warm skim milk in a mixing bowl. Crumble 1/2 oz. of fresh yeast and stir. Add 1 1/2 teas. salt, 1 tables. honey and 3 cups of unbleached white flour. Combine thoroughly, using a wooden spoon.

Put 1 1/2 cups of white flour on a dough board. Set the dough in the center. The next step calls for hard kneading, since this is an especially firm dough. Knead until the flour is mixed. Shape into a round bread. Allow this formula to rise in a warm place for about 20 to 30 minutes, or until quite light.

Set the bread in an oiled shallow baking pan 8 1/2 × 11 × 1 1/2". Preheat oven at 350° and bake for about 1 hour, until a light golden color. Check with a wire tester. Cool on a rack.